D0024983

REF

The American Revolution

GOLDENTREE BIBLIOGRAPHIES
IN AMERICAN HISTORY

under the series editorship of
ARTHUR S. LINK

FORTHCOMING TITLES

MAI 16 1974

908-1B-98

The American Revolution

compiled by

John Shy

The University of Michigan

 AHM PUBLISHING CORPORATION
Northbrook, Illinois 60062

348892

Copyright © 1973
AHM PUBLISHING CORPORATION

All rights reserved

This book, or parts thereof, must not be used or reproduced in any manner without written permission. For information address the publisher, AHM PUBLISHING CORPORATION, 1500 Skokie Boulevard, Northbrook, Illinois 60062.

ISBN: 0-88295-532-2

E
208
.Z9
S468
1973

Library of Congress Card Number: 72-178292

PRINTED IN THE UNITED STATES OF AMERICA

713-1

Editor's Foreword

GOLDENTREE BIBLIOGRAPHIES IN AMERICAN HISTORY are designed to provide students, teachers, and librarians with ready and reliable guides to the literature of American History in all its remarkable scope and variety. Volumes in the series cover comprehensively the major periods in American history, while additional volumes are devoted to all important subjects.

Goldentree Bibliographies attempt to steer a middle course between the brief list of references provided in the average textbook and the long bibliography in which significant items are often lost in the sheer number of titles listed. Each bibliography is, therefore, selective, with the sole criterion for choice being the significance—and not the age—of any particular work. The result is bibliographies of all works, including journal articles and doctoral dissertations, that are still useful, without bias in favor of any particular historiographical school.

Each compiler is a scholar long associated, both in research and teaching, with the period or subject of his volume. All compilers have not only striven to accomplish the objective of this series but have also cheerfully adhered to a general style and format. However, each compiler has been free to define his field, make his own selections, and work out internal organization as the unique demands of his period or subject have seemed to dictate.

The single great objective of *Goldentree Bibliographies in American History* will have been achieved if these volumes help researchers and students to find their way to the significant literature of American history.

Arthur S. Link

Preface

TO CONFINE A phenomenon like the American Revolution within a pair of dates inevitably distorts it. Did the Revolution "begin" in 1763? Did it "end" in 1783? A bibliography that seeks, as this one does, to be fair and representative must leave these questions open. Thus the editor has wisely and generously permitted me to range beyond the conventional limits to select from the colonial and early national periods work that illuminates the origins and outcome of the Revolution. No attempt, however, has been made to deal comprehensively with American history before 1763 and after 1783, and the other bibliographies in the series should be consulted for complete coverage beyond those dates.

The arrangement of material within each section is, in general, alphabetical by author. There are several exceptions: bibliographical articles, where they exist, are at the head of the appropriate section; and works that review or discuss other specific works are usually located immediately following the work under discussion. The biographical sections are alphabetized by subject, and the section on military operations is arranged to follow the chronology of the war. A few unpublished dissertations are listed in cases where published monographic work is relatively unsatisfactory, and some major collections of printed sources have earned inclusion by their enduring value and influence. There are cross-references to the most important items, and a few are simply listed twice for convenience, but for any topic all the obviously related sections should be consulted. In this respect, biography and local history deserve special notice, because often such work does not fit easily into any other analytical category and yet is especially relevant to several categories. Charles H. Lesser was a valuable assistant in checking and indexing the bibliography.

A final brief word on the state of the subject itself seems in order: after 1775 or 1776, there is a distinct drop in the quality, quantity, and range of published research; not until the question of the Constitution imposes itself on historical consciousness does the level again rise to that of the work done on the coming of the Revolution. Of course there are notable exceptions, with the books of Merrill Jensen and Allan Nevins coming perhaps most readily to mind; the Loyalists, military operations, and wartime diplomacy have each received an enormous amount of attention. But surprisingly large areas of ignorance remain, and in general the war and its immediate aftermath constitute the neglected period of the American Revolution.

J. S.

Abbreviations

Ag Hist	Agricultural History
Am	Americana
Am Ecc Rev	American Ecclesiastical Review
Am Geneal	American Genealogist
Am Hist Rev	American Historical Review
Am J Leg Hist	American Journal of Legal History
Am Jew Arch	American Jewish Archives
Am Lit	American Literature; A Journal of Literary History, Criticism and Bibliography
Am Neptune	American Neptune; A Quarterly Journal of Maritime History
Am Ox	American Oxonian (Alumni Association of American Rhodes Scholars)
Am Pol Sci Rev	American Political Science Review
Am Q	American Quarterly
Am Soc Rev	American Sociological Review
Annales	Annales. Economies, Societes, Civilisations
Ann Med Hist	Annals of Medical History
Ann Rep Am Hist Assn	Annual Report, American Historical Association
ASI	Archivio Storico Italiano
Bermuda Hist Q	Bermuda Historical Quarterly
Bos Pub Lib Q	Boston Public Library Quarterly
Bull Brit Assn Am Stud	Bulletin of the British Association of American Studies
Bull Conn Hist Soc	Bulletin, Connecticut Historical Society
Bull Econ Pol Sci Hist Ser (Wis)	Bulletin, Economics, Political Science, and History Series, University of Wisconsin
Bull Inst Hist Res	Bulletin of the Institute of Historical Research
Bull J Ry Lib	Bulletin, John Rylands Library
Bull N-Y Hist Soc	Bulletin of the New-York History Society
Bull N Y Pub Lib	Bulletin, New York Public Library
Bull O St Univ	Bulletin, Ohio State University
Bull Westchester County Hist Soc	Bulletin, Westchester County Historical Society
Bus Hist Rev	Business History Review
Canad J Econ Pol Sci	Canadian Journal of Economics, Politics, and Science

Canad Hist Rev	Canadian Historical Review
Ch Hist	Church History
Chron Okla	Chronicles of Oklahoma
Cithara	Cithara: Essays in the Judeo-Christian Tradition
Clas J	Classical Journal
Coll Mass Hist Soc	Collections, Massachusetts Historical Society
Coll N-Y Hist Soc	Collections, New-York Historical Society
Columbia Univ Q	Columbia University Quarterly
Comp Stud Hist Soc	Comparative Studies in History and Society
Dal Rev	Dalhousie Review
Del Hist	Delaware History
Econ Hist Rev	Economic History Review
Emory Univ Q	Emory University Quarterly
Eng Hist Rev	English Historical Review
Essex Inst Hist Coll	Essex Institute Historical Collections
Explor Entrep Hist	Explorations in Entrepreneurial History
Fla Hist Q	Florida Historical Quarterly
French Hist Stud	French Historical Studies
Ga Hist Q	Georgia Historical Quarterly
Geog Rev	Geographical Review
Har Alum Bull	Harvard Alumni Bulletin
His-Am Hist Rev	Hispanic-American Historical Review
Hist Mag P E Ch	Historical Magazine of the Protestant Episcopal Church
Hist Today	History Today
Hist Theory	History and Theory
Hist Zeit	Historische Zeitschrift
Hostorian	The Historian: A Journal of History
Hunt Lib Bull	Huntington Library Bulletin
Hunt Lib Q	The Huntington Library Quarterly: A Journal for the History and Interpretation of English Civilization
Ill Law Rev	Illinois Law Review
Ind Mag Hist	Indiana Magazine of History
Int Rev Soc Hist	International Review of Social History
Irish Hist Stud	Irish Historical Studies
J Am Hist	Journal of American History
J Am Mil Inst	Journal, American Military Institute
J Am Inst Crim Law	Journal, American Institute of Criminal Law
J Brit Stud	The Journal of British Studies
J Ch St	Journal of Church and State
J Ecc Hist	Journal of Ecclesiastical History
J Econ Bus Hist	Journal of Economic and Business History
J Econ Hist	Journal of Economic History
J Hist Ideas	Journal of the History of Ideas
J Ill St Hist Soc	Journal of the Illinois State Historical Society

J Mod Hist	Journal of Modern History
J Neg Hist	The Journal of Negro History
J N Y St Hist Assn	Journal of the New York State Historical Association
J Pol	Journal of Politics
J Presby Hist Soc	Journal, Presbyterian Historical Society
J Q	Journalism Quarterly
J Roy Un Serv Inst	Journal, Royal United Service Institution
J S Hist	The Journal of Southern History
J Soc Army Hist Res	Journal of the Society for Army Historical Research
J Soc Hist	Journal of Social HistoryoLabor History
Labor Hist	Louisiana Historical Quarterly
La Hist Q	Library Quarterly, A Journal of Investigation and Discussion in the Field of Library Science
Lib Q	
Mag Hist	Magazine of History, with Notes and Queries
Md Hist Mag	Maryland Historical Magazine
Mich Alum Q Rev	Michigan Alumni Quarterly Review
Mil Affairs	Military Affairs
Miss Val Hist Rev	Mississippi Valley Historical Review: A Journal of American History; *continued as* The Journal of American History
More Books	*(Predecessor of* Bos Pub Lib Q*)*
N C Booklet	North Carolina Booklet
N C Hist Rev	North Carolina Historical Review
N Eng Hist Geneal Reg	New England Historical and Genealogical Register
N Eng Q	New England Quarterly: An Historical Review of the New England Life and Letters
N J Hist	New Jersey History
N Y Hist	New York History *(New York State Historical Association)*
N-Y Hist Soc Q	New-York Historical Society Quarterly Bulletin
N Y St Hist Assn Q J	New York State Historical Association Quarterly Journal
Old-Time N Eng	Old-Time New England
Ontario Hist	Ontario History
Pa Hist	Pennsylvania History
Pa Mag Hist	Pennsylvania Magazine of History and Biography
Pac Hist Rev	Pacific Historical Review
Pap Bibliog Soc Am	Papers, Bibliographical Society of America
Pap Mich Ac Sc Ar Let	Papers, Michigan Academy of Science, Arts and Letters
Pap N Haven Col Hist Soc	Papers, New Haven Colony Historical Society
Pap Ontario Hist Soc	Papers, Ontario Historical Society

Pap Richmond Col Hist	Richmond College Historical Papers
Past Pres	Past and Present; Studies in the History of Civilization
Pol Sci Q	Political Science Quarterly
Proc Am Ant Soc	Proceedings, American Antiquarian Society
Proc Am Philos Soc	Proceedings of the American Philosophical Society
Proc Bunker Hill Mon Assn	Proceedings, Bunker Hill Monument Association
Proc Mass Hist Soc	Proceedings, Massachusetts Historical Society
Proc N J Hist Soc	Proceedings, New Jersey Historical Society
Proc N Y St Hist Assn	Proceedings, New York State Historical Association
Proc S C Hist Assn	Proceedings, South Carolina Historical Association
Proc Ulster County Hist Soc	Proceedings, Ulster County Historical Association
Pub Col Soc Mass	Publications, Colonial Society of Massachusetts
Pub E Tenn Hist Soc	Publications, East Tennessee Historical Society
Pub Miss Hist Assn	Publications, Mississippi Historical Association
Pub O Arch Hist Soc	Publications, Ohio Archaeological and Historical Society
Pub Roch Hist Soc	Publication Fund Series, Rochester Historical Society
Pub Worcester Hist Soc	Publications, Worcester Historical Society
Q J Econ	Quarterly Journal of Economics
Q J Sp	Quarterly Journal of Speech
Q Rev	Quarterly Review
Ren Mod Stud	Renaissance and Modern Studies
Rev Pol	The Review of Politics
R I Hist	Rhode Island History
R I Hist Soc Coll	Rhode Island Historical Society Collections
Roy Soc Canad Trans	Royal Society of Canada, Transactions
S Atl Q	South Atlantic Quarterly
School Rev	The School Review: A Journal of Secondary Education
Scot Hist Rev	Scottish History Review
S C Hist Mag	South Carolina Historical Magazine
S C Law Q	South Carolina Law Quarterly
Slav Rev	Slavic Review
Smithsonian J Hist	Smithsonian Journal of History
Soc Ser Rev	The Social Service Review: A Quarterly Devoted to the Scientific and Professional Interests of Social Work
Soc Stud	Social Studies

Stud Hist Econ Pub Law (Colum)	Studies in History, Economics, and Public Law, *Columbia University*
Stud Hist Pol Sci (Hop)	Studies in History and Political Science, *Johns Hopkins University*
Stud Hist (Smith)	Studies in History, *Smith College*
Trans Stud Phila Col Phy	Transactions and Studies, Philadelphia College of Physicians
Tyler's Q Hist Gen Mag	Tyler's Quarterly Historical and Genealogical Magazine
U Birmingham Hist J	University of Birmingham Historical Journal
U S Cath Hist Soc Rec	U.S. Catholic Historical Society, Historical Records and Studies
Va Mag Hist	Virginia Magazine of History and Biography
Vt Hist	Vermont History
W Pa Hist Mag	Western Pennsylvania Historical Magazine
W Va Hist	West Virginia History, A Quarterly Magazine
Wm Mar Q	William and Mary Quarterly
Wor Pol	World Politics

Note: Cross-references are to page and item number. Items marked by a dagger (†) are available in paperback edition at the time this bibliography goes to press. The publisher and compiler invite suggestions for additions to future editions of the bibliography.

Contents

I. Bibliographies and Guides

1 ADAMS, Thomas R. *American Independence: The Growth of an Idea. A Bibliographic Study of the American Political Pamphlets Printed Between 1764 and 1776 Dealing with the Dispute Between Great Britain and Her Colonies.* Providence, 1965.

2 ADAMS, Thomas R. "The British Pamphlets of the American Revolution for 1774: A Progress Report." *Proc Mass Hist Soc*, LXXXI (1969), 31-103.

3 BAILYN, Bernard. *Education in the Forming of American Society: Needs and Opportunities for Study.* Chapel Hill, 1960.

4 BEERS, Henry P. *Bibliographies in American History? Guide to Materials for Research.* Rev. ed. New York, 1942.

5 BELL, Whitfield J. *Early American Science: Needs and Opportunities for Study.* Williamsburg, 1955.

6 BRADFORD, Thomas L., and S. V. HENKELS. *The Bibliographer's Manual of American History, Containing an Account of All State, Territory, Town and County Histories* . . . . 3 vols. Philadelphia, 1907-1910.

7 BRIGHAM, Clarence S. *History and Bibliography of American Newspapers, 1690-1820.* 2 vols. Worcester, Mass., 1947.

8 BRIGHAM, Clarence S. "Additions and Corrections to History and Bibliography of American Newspapers, 1690-1820." *Proc Am Ant Soc*, n.s., LXXI (1961), 15-62.

9 CLARK, Thomas D. *Travels in the Old South: A Bibliography.* 2 vols. Norman, Okla., 1956.

10 DANIELS, Lorna M. *Studies in Enterprise: A Selected Bibliography of American and Canadian Company Histories and Biographies of Businessmen.* Cambridge, Mass., 1957.

11 EVANS, Charles. *American Bibliography.* Repr. 14 vols. Worcester, Mass., 1941-1959.

12 FAY, Bernard. *Bibliographie Critique des Ouvrages Français relatifs aux Etats-Unis (1770-1800).* Paris, 1925.

13 FENTON, William N. *American Indian and White Relations to 1830.* Chapel Hill, 1957.

14 FORBES, Harriette M. *New England Diaries, 1602-1800.* Topsfield, Mass., 1923.

15 GIPSON, Lawrence H. *A Bibliographical Guide to the History of the British Empire, 1748-1776.* Vol. XIV of *The British Empire Before the American Revolution.* New York, 1969.

16 HARPER, Lawrence A. "Recent Contributions to American Economic History: American History to 1789." *J Econ Hist*, XIX (1959), 1-24.

1 Harvard University Library. *Widener Library Shelflist, nos. 9-13: American History.* 5 vols. Cambridge, Mass., 1967.

2 HECHT, J. Jean. "The Reign of George III in Recent Historiography: A Bibliographical Essay." *Bull N Y Pub Lib*, LXX (1966), 279-304.

3 HIGGS, Henry. *Bibliography of Economics, 1751-1775.* Cambridge, 1935.

4 HINDLE, Brooke. *Technology in Early America: Needs and Opportunities for Study.* Chapel Hill, 1966.

5 *International Bibliography of Historical Sciences.* 35 vols., in progress. Paris, 1926- .

6 JENSEN, Merrill. *American Colonial Documents to 1776.* Vol. IX of *English Historical Documents.* New York, 1955.

7 KUEHL, Warren F. *Dissertations in History: An Index to Dissertations Completed in History Departments of United States and Canadian Universities, 1873-1960.* Lexington, Ky., 1965.

8 LARNED, Josephus N. *The Literature of American History, A Bibliographic Guide . . . .* Boston, 1902.

9 MATTHEWS, William. *American Diaries: An Annotated Bibliography of American Diaries Written Prior to the Year 1861.* Berkeley, 1945.

10 MATTHEWS, William. *British Autobiographies: An Annotated Bibliography of British Autobiographies Published or Written Before 1951.* Berkeley, 1955.

11 MATTHEWS, William. *British Diaries: An Annotated Bibliography of British Diaries Written Between 1442 and 1942.* Berkeley, 1950.

12 MERENESS, Newton D. *Travels in the American Colonies.* New York, 1916.

13 MONAGHAN, Frank. *French Travellers in the U.S., 1765-1932.* New York, 1933.

14 PARGELLIS, Stanley M., and D. J. MEDLEY. *Bibliography of British History. The Eighteenth Century, 1714-1789.* Oxford, 1951.

15 PETERSON, Clarence S. *Bibliography of Local Histories in the Atlantic States.* Baltimore, 1966.

16 PORTER, Dorothy Burnett, "Early Negro Writings; A Bibliographical Study." *Bibliographical Society of America, Papers,* XXXIX (1945), 192-268.

17 RAGATZ, Lowell J. *A Guide for Study of British Caribbean History, 1763-1834.* Washington, D.C., 1933.

18 RAGATZ, Lowell J. *A List of Books and Articles on Colonial History and Overseas Expansion Published in the United States.* London, 1939.

19 RICHARDSON, Lyon N. *A History of Early American Magazines, 1741-1789.* New York, 1931.

1 ROOS, Frank J. *Writings on Early American Architecture: An Annotated List of Books and Articles on Architecture Constructed before 1860 . . . .* Columbus, Ohio, 1943.

2 SABIN, Joseph A. *Bibliotheca Americana. A Dictionary of Books Relating to America from Its Discovery to the Present Time.* 29 vols. New York, 1868-1936.

3 WILLIAMS, Judith Blow. *A Guide to the Printed Materials for English Social and Economic History, 1750-1850.* 2 vols. New York, 1926.

4 WINSOR, Justin H. *Narrative and Critical History of America*, Vols. V-VII. Boston and New York, 1887-1888.

5 WINSOR, Justin H. *Reader's Handbook of the American Revolution, 1761-83.* Boston, 1880.

6 *Writings on American History, 1902-* . Ed. Grace G. Griffin and others. New York, Washington, D.C., New Haven, and Princeton, 1904- .

7 *Writings on British History (1934-1945).* Ed. A. Taylor Milne. London, 1937-1960.

II. General Works

1. Historiography

8 BAILYN, Bernard. "Becker, Andrews, and the Image of Colonial Origins." *N Eng Q*, (1965), 522-534.

9 BEALE, Howard K., ed. *Charles A. Beard.* Lexington, Ky., 1954.

10 BORNING, Bernard C. *The Political and Social Thought of Charles A. Beard.* New York, 1962.

11 CRAVEN, Wesley Frank. *The Legend of the Founding Fathers.* New York, 1956.†

12 CRAVEN, Wesley Frank. "The Revolutionary Era." In *The Reconstruction of American History*, ed. John Higham. New York, 1963.

13 EISENSTADT, A. S. *Charles McLean Andrews.* New York, 1956.

14 GIPSON, Lawrence H. "Historiography." Vol. XIII, Pt. III, of *The British Empire Before the American Revolution.* New York, 1968.

15 GIPSON, Lawrence H. "The Imperial Approach to Early American History." In *The Reinterpretation of Early American History*, ed. R. A. Billington. San Marino, Calif., 1966.

16 GREENE, Jack P. *The Reappraisal of the American Revolution in Recent Historical Literature.* Washington, D.C., 1967.

17 GREENE, Jack P., ed. *The Reinterpretation of the American Revolution.* New York, 1967.†

1 JAMESON, J. Franklin. *The History of Historical Writing in America.* Boston, 1891.

2 JENSEN, Merrill. "Historians and the Nature of the American Revolution." In *The Reinterpretation of Early American History*, ed. R. A. Billington. San Marino, Calif., 1966.

3 MARSHALL, Peter. "Radicals, Conservatives, and the American Revolution." *Past Pres*, No. 23 (1962), 44-56.

4 MASON, Bernard. "The Heritage of Carl Becker." *N-Y Hist Soc Q*, LIII (1969), 127-147.

5 MORGAN, Edmund S. *The American Revolution: A Review of Changing Interpretations.* Washington, D.C., 1958.

6 MORGAN, Edmund S. "The American Revolution: Revisions in Need of Revising." *Wm Mar Q*, 3d ser., XIV (1957), 3-15.

7 MORRIS, Richard B. "Class Struggle and the American Revolution." *Wm Mar Q*, 3d ser., XIX (1962), 3-29.

8 RIEMER, Neal. "Two Conceptions of the Genius of American Politics." *J Pol*, XX (1958), 695-717.

9 SCHLESINGER, Arthur M. *In Retrospect: The History of a Historian.* New York, 1963.

10 SMITH, William R. *History as Argument: Three Patriot Historians of the American Revolution.* The Hague, 1966. (On Ramsay, Warren, and Marshall.)

11 VAN TASSEL, David D. *Recording America's Past; An Interpretation of the Development of Historical Studies in America, 1607-1884.* Chicago, 1960.

12 WILKINS, Burleigh T. *Carl Becker.* Cambridge, Mass., 1961.†

13 WINKS, Robin, ed. *The Historiography of the British Empire-Commonwealth: Trends, Interpretations, and Resources.* Durham, N.C., 1966.

14 WOOD, Gordon. "Rhetoric and Reality in the American Revolution." *Wm Mar Q*, 3d ser., XXIII (1966), 3-32.

15 WRIGHT, Esmond. *The American Revolution.* Leicester, Eng., 1967.†

2. Surveys and Interpretative Essays

16 ADAMS, James T. *Revolutionary New England, 1691-1776.* Boston, 1923.

17 ALDEN, John. *The South in the Revolution, 1763-1789.* Baton Rouge, 1957.

18 "The American Revolution: A Symposium." *Canad Hist Rev*, XXIII (1942), 1-41.

19 ANDREWS, Charles M. "The American Revolution: An Interpretation.: *Am Hist Rev*, XXXI (1925-1926), 219-232.

1 ANDREWS, Charles M. *The Colonial Background of the American Revolution, Four Essays in American Colonial History.* Rev. ed. New Haven, 1931.†

2 APTHEKER, Herbert. *The American Revolution, 1763-1783.* New York, 1960.†

3 BANCROFT, George. *History of the United States of America.* 10 vols. Boston, 1834-1874; rev. ed., 6 vols., Boston, 1876.

4 BARROW, Thomas C. "The American Revolution as a Colonial War for Independence." *Wm Mar Q*, 3d ser., XXV (1968), 452-464.

5 BECKER, Carl L. *The Eve of the Revolution: A Chronicle of the Breach with England.* New Haven, 1918.

6 BECKER, Carl L., J. M. CLARK, and W. E. DODD. *The Spirit of '76 and Other Essays.* Washington, D.C., 1927.

7 BOTTA, Carlo. *History of the War of Independence of the U.S.A.* 3 vols. Philadelphia, 1820.

8 CHALMERS, George. *An Introduction to the History of the Revolt of the American Colonies.* 2 vols. Boston, 1845.

9 CHANNING, Edward. *The American Revolution, 1761-1789.* Vol. III of *A History of the United States.* New York, 1912.

10 CROSSMAN, R. H. S. "The American Revolution." In *Government and the Governed.* London, 1940.

11 DARLING, Arthur B. *Our Rising Empire, 1763-1803.* New Haven, 1940.

12 EGERTON, H. E. *The Causes and Character of the American Revolution.* Oxford, 1923.

13 FERRARI, Aldo. "La rivoluzione Nord-Americana (1760-1790)." *Rivista d'Italia*, XXIV (1929), 425-438.

14 FISHER, Sydney G. *The Struggle for American Independence.* 2 vols. London and Philadelphia, 1908.

15 FISKE, John. *The American Revolution.* 2 vols. Boston, 1891.

16 GIBBES, Robert W., ed. *Documentary History of the American Revolution . . . .* 3 vols. New York, 1855-1857.

17 GIPSON, Lawrence H. *The British Empire Before the American Revolution.* 14 vols., in progress. New York, 1936- .

18 LOWRER, A. R. M. "Lawrence H. Gipson and the First British Empire: An Evaluation." *J Brit Stud*, III (1963), 57-58.

19 MORRIS, Richard B. "The Spacious Empire of Lawrence Henry Gipson." *Wm Mar Q*, 3d ser., XXIV (1967), 168-189.

20 GOODWIN, A., ed. *The American and French Revolution, 1763-1793.* Vol. VIII of *The New Cambridge Modern History.* Cambridge, 1965.

1　GORDON, William. *The History of the Rise, Progress, and Establishment of the Independence of the United States* . . . . 4 vols. London 1788.

2　LIBBY, Orin G. "A Critical Examination of Gordon's History of the American Revolution." *Ann Rep Am Hist Assn*, I (1899), 367-388.

3　GREENE, Evarts B. *The Revolutionary Generation, 1763-1790.* New York, 1943.

4　HACKER, Louis M. "The First American Revolution." *Columbia Univ Q*, XXVII (1935), 259-295.

5　HARLOW, Vincent T, and F. M. MADDEN. *The Founding of the Second British Empire, 1763-1793.* 2 vols. London, 1951-1964.

6　HARTZ, Louis. *The Liberal Tradition in America.* New York, 1955.†

7　HAUSER, Henri. "De Quelques Aspects de la Révolution Américaine." *Révolution Française*, LXXIV (1921), 193-210.

8　JENSEN, Merrill. "The American People and the American Revolution." *J Am Hist*, LVII (1970), 5-35.

9　JENSEN, Merrill. "Democracy and the American Revolution." *Hunt Lib Q*, XX (1956-1957), 321-341.

10　KELLER, Hans G. *Die Wurzeln der Amerikanischen Demokratie.* Bern, 1958.

11　KENYON, Cecilia M. "Republicanism and Radicalism in the American Revolution: An Old-fashioned Interpretation." *Wm Mar Q*, 3d ser., XIX (1962), 143-182.

12　LACY, Dan. *The Meaning of the American Revolution.* New York, 1964.†

13　LECKY, W. E. H. *The American Revolution, 1763-1783.* Boston and New York, 1898.

14　LEMISCH, Jesse. "The American Revolution Seen from the Bottom up." In *Towards a New Past*, ed. Barton J. Bernstein. New York, 1968.

15　LYND, Staughton. *Class Conflict, Slavery, and the United States Constitution.* Indianapolis, 1967.

16　MC LAUGHLIN, Andrew C. "Some Reflections on the American Revolution." In *Aspects of the Social History of America*, by T. Sizer and others. Chapel Hill, 1931.

17　MAIN, Jackson T. *The Upper House in Revolutionary America, 1763-1788.* Madison, 1967.

18　MOORE, Frank, ed. *Diary of the American Revolution, from Newspapers and Original Documents.* 2 vols. New York, 1860.†

19　MORGAN, Edmund S. *The Birth of the Republic, 1763-89.* Chicago, 1956.†

20　MORGAN, Edmund S. "The Puritan Ethic and the American Revolution." *Wm Mar Q*, 3d ser., XXIV (1967), 3-43.

21　MORISON, Samuel E., ed. *Sources and Documents Illustrating the American Revolution.* 2d ed. Oxford and New York, 1965.†

1 MORRIS, Richard B. *The American Revolution Reconsidered.* New York, 1967.†

2 MORRIS, Richard B. "Class Struggle and the American Revolution." *Wm Mar Q*, 3d ser., XIX (1962), 3-29.

3 MORRIS, Richard B., ed. *The Era of the American Revolution: Studies Inscribed to Evarts Boutell Greene.* New York, 1939.

4 NEVINS, Allan. *The American States During and After the Revolution, 1775-1789.* New York, 1924.

5 NILES, Hezekiah, ed. *Principles and Acts of the Revolution in America.* Baltimore, 1822; re-ed. by Alden T. Vaughan under the title *Chronicles of the American Revolution*, New York, 1965.†

6 OSGOOD, Herbert L. "The American Revolution." *Pol Sci Q*, XIII (1898), 41-59.

7 PFISTER, A. *Amerikanische Revolution, 1775-1783.* 2 vols. Stuttgart, 1904.

8 RAMSAY, David. *The History of the American Revolution.* Philadelphia, 1789.

9 SMITH, Page. "David Ramsay and the Causes of the American Revolution." *Wm Mar Q*, 3d ser., XVII (1960), 51-77.

10 RAYNAL, Guillaume T. *Révolution de l'Amérique.* London, 1781. (Numerous eds. in English.)

11 RITCHESON, Charles R. *British Politics and the American Revolution.* Norman, Okla., 1954.

12 ROBSON, Eric. *The American Revolution in Its Political and Military Aspects, 1763-1783.* London and New York, 1955.†

13 ROSE, J. Holland, A. P. NEWTON, and E. A. BENIANS. *The Cambridge History of the British Empire.* Vols. I and VI. Cambridge, 1929-1930.

14 SPIEGEL, Käthe. "Kulturgeschichtliche Grundlagen der Amerikanischen Revolution." *Hist Zeit*, Beiheft 21 (1931).

15 STEDMAN, Charles. *The History of the Origin, Progress and Termination of the American War.* 2 vols. Dublin and London, 1794.

16 NEWMYER, R. Ken. "Charles Stedman's *History of the American War*." *Am Hist Rev*, LXIII (1957-1958), 924-234.

17 TREVELYAN, Sir George O. *The American Revolution.* 4 vols. New York, 1899-1907.

18 TREVELYAN, Sir George O. *George the Third and Charles Fox, the Concluding Part of the American Revolution.* 2 vols. New York, 1912-1914.

19 U.S. Bureau of the Census. *Historical Statistics of the United States, Colonial Times to 1957.* Washington, D.C., 1960.

1 VAN TYNE, Claude H. *The Causes of the War of Independence.* Boston and New York, 1922.

2 VAN TYNE, Claude H. *The War of Independence, American Phase.* Boston and New York, 1929.

3 WARREN, Mercy Otis. *History of the Rise, Progress and Termination of the American Revolution.* 3 vols. Boston, 1805.

4 WATSON, Steven J. *The Reign of George III, 1760-1815.* Oxford, 1960.

5 WILLIAMS, William. "The Age of Mercantilism: An Interpretation of the American Political Economy, 1763-1828." *Wm Mar Q*, 3d ser., XV (1958), 419-437.

6 WRIGHT, Esmond. *Fabric of Freedom, 1763-1800.* New York, 1961.

7 WRIGHT, Esmond, ed. *Causes and Consequences of the American Revolution.* Chicago, 1966.†

III. Colonial Society on the Eve of Revolutionary Conflict

1. In General

8 BOORSTIN, Daniel J. *The Americans: The Colonial Experience.* New York, 1958.†

9 BRIDENBAUGH, Carl. *Cities in Revolt: Urban Life in America, 1743-1776.* New York, 1955†

10 BRIDENBAUGH, Carl. *Myths and Realities; Societies of the Colonial South.* Baton Rouge, 1952.†

11 HAWKE, David. *The Colonial Experience.* Indianapolis, 1966.

12 JONES, Howard M. *O Strange New World. American Culture: The Formative Years.* New York, 1964.†

13 POTTER, David. *People of Plenty: Economic Abundance and the American Character.* Chicago, 1958.†

14 SACHS, William S., and Ari HOOGENBOOM. *The Enterprising Colonials: Society on the Eve of the Revolution.* Chicago, 1965.

15 SCHLESINGER, Arthur M. *The Birth of the Nation: A Portrait of the American People on the Eve of Independence.* New York, 1968.

16 VER STEEG, Clarence L. *The Formative Years, 1607-1763.* New York, 1964.

2. Family and Demographic Structure

17 BENSON, Mary S. *Women in Eighteen-Century America; A Study of Opinion and Social Usage.* New York, 1935.

1   CALHOUN, Arthur W. *A Social History of the American Family from Colonial Times to the Present.* 3 vols. Cleveland, 1917-1919.

2   FLEMING, Sandford. *Children and Puritanism, the Place of Children in the Life and Thought of New England Churches, 1620-1847.* New Haven, 1933.

3   FRIIS, Herman R. *A Series of Population Maps of the Colonies and the United States, 1625-1790.* New York, 1940.

4   GREENE, Evarts B., and Virginia D. HARRINGTON. *American Population Before the Federal Census of 1790.* New York, 1932.

5   GREVEN, Philip J., Jr. "Family Structure in Seventeenth-Century Andover, Massachusetts." *Wm Mar Q*, 3d ser., XXIII (1966), 234-256.

6   GREVEN, Philip J., Jr. *Four Generations: Land and Family in Colonial Andover, Massachusetts.* Ithaca, N.Y., 1970.

7   JACOBUS, Donald L. "Age of Girls at Marriage in Colonial New England." *Am Geneal*, XXVII (1951), 116-118.

8   KEIM, C. Ray. "Primogeniture and Entail in Colonial Virginia." *Wm Mar Q*, 3d ser., XXV (1968), 545-586.

9   KIEFER, Monica M. "Early American Childhood in the Middle Atlantic Area." *Pa Mag Hist*, LXVIII (1944), 3-37.

10 LEONARD, Eugenie Andruss, et al. *The American Woman in Colonial and Revolutionary Times, 1565-1800: A Syllabus with Bibliography.* Philadelphia, 1962.

11 MERRENS, H. Roy. "Historical Geography and Early American History." *Wm Mar Q*, 3d ser., XXII (1965), 529-548.

12 MOLLER, Herbert. "Sex Composition and Correlated Culture Patterns of Colonial America." *Wm Mar Q*, 3d ser., II (1945), 113-153.

13 MORGAN, Edmund S. *Virginians at Home: Family Life in the Eighteenth Century.* Williamsburg, 1952.†

14 OLSEN, Albert L. *Agricultural Economy and the Population in Eighteenth-Century Connecticut.* New Haven, 1935.

15 POTTER, J. "The Growth of Population in America, 1700-1860." In *Population in History, Essays in Historical Demography*, ed. D. V. Glass and D. E. C. Eversley. Chicago, 1965.

16 ROTHMAN, David J. "A Note on the Study of the Colonial Family." *Wm Mar Q*, 3d ser., XXIII (1966), 627-634.

17 ROSSITER, W. S. *A Century of Population Growth.* Washington, D.C., 1909.

18 SPRUILL, Julia Cherry. *Women's Life and Work in the Southern Colonies.* Chapel Hill, 1938.

19 STEVENSON, Noel C. "Marital Rights in the Colonial Period." *N Eng Hist Geneal Reg*, CIX (1955), 84-90.

20 SUTHERLAND, Stella H. *Population Distritubion in Colonial America.* New York, 1936.

3. Social Structure

A. CLASS, STATUS, AND OCCUPATION

1 BRIDENBAUGH, Carl. "Baths and Watering Places of Colonial America." *Wm Mar Q*, 3d ser., III (1946), 151-181.

2 BRIDENBAUGH, Carl. *The Colonial Craftsman.* New York, 1950.†

3 BRIDENBAUGH, Carl. *Peter Harrison: First American Architect.* Chapel Hill, 1949.

4 CHROUST, Anton-Hermann. *The Rise of the Legal Profession in America.* 2 vols. Norman, Okla., 1965.

5 DILLON, Dorothy. *The New York Triumvirate: A Study of the Legal and Political Careers of William Livingston, John Morin Scott, William Smith, Jr.* New York, 1949.

6 EATON, Clement. "A Mirror of the Southern Colonial Lawyer: The Fee Books of Patrick Henry, Thomas Jefferson and Waightstill Avery." *Wm Mar Q*, 3d Ser., VIII (1951), 520-534.

7 EVANS, Emory G. "The Rise and Decline of the Virginia Aristocracy in the Eighteenth Century: The Nelsons." In *The Old Dominion*, ed. Darrett B. Rutman. Charlottesville, Va., 1964.

8 FREIBERG, Malcolm. "Thomas Hutchinson: The First Fifty Years (1711-1761)." *Wm Mar Q*, 3d ser., XV (1958), 35-55. See 76.1.

9 GREENE, Jack P. "Foundations of Political Power in the Virginia House of Burgesses, 1720-1776." *Wm Mar Q*, 3d ser., XVI (1959), 485-506.

10 HEDGES, James Blaine. *The Browns of Providence Plantations: Colonial Years.* Cambridge, Mass., 1952.

11 HINDLE, Brooke. "A Colonial Governor's Family: The Coldens of Coldengham." *N-Y Hist Soc Q*, XLV (1961), 233-250.

12 HUTSON, James H. "An Investigation of the Inarticulate: Philadelphia's White Oaks." *Wm Mar Q*, 3d ser., XXVIII (1971), 3-25.

13 JERNEGAN, Marcus W. *Laboring and Dependent Classes in Colonial America . . . .* Chicago, 1931.

14 KIMBALL, Fiske. *Domestic Architecture of the American Colonies and of the Early Republic.* New York, 1922.†

15 KLEIN, Milton M. "The Rise of the New York Bar: The Legal Career of William Livingston." *Wm Mar Q*, 3d ser., XV (1958), 334-358.

16 LABAREE, Leonard W. *Conservatism in Early American History.* New York, 1948.†

17 LAND, Aubrey C. "Economic Base and Social Structure: The Northern Chesapeake in the Eighteenth Century." *J Econ Hist*, XXV (1965), 639-654.

1   LEMISCH, Jesse. "Jack Tar in the Streets: Merchant Seamen in the Politics of Revolutionary America." *Wm Mar Q*, 3d ser., XXV (1968), 371-407.

2   MC ANEAR, Beverly. "The Place of Freemen in Old New York." *N Y Hist*, XXI (1940), 418-430.

3   MAIN, Jackson T. "The One Hundred." *Wm Mar Q*, 3d ser., XI (1954), 354-384.

4   MAIN, Jackson T. *The Social Structure of Revolutionary America*. Princeton, 1965.

5   MARCUS, Jacob R. *Early American Jewry*. 2 vols. Philadelphia, 1951-1953.

6   MAYS, David J. *Edmund Pendleton, 1721-1803*. 2 vols. Cambridge, Mass., 1952.

7   MORRIS, Richard B. *Government and Labor in Early America*. New York, 1946.†

8   MORTON, Louis. *Robert Carter of Nomini Hall: A Virginia Tobacco Planter of the Eighteenth Century*. Williamsburg, 1941.†

9   OWINGS, Donnell M. *His Lordship's Patronage: Offices of Profit in Colonial Maryland*. Baltimore, 1953.

10 PARKER, Peter J. "The Philadelphia Printer: A Study of an Eighteenth-Century Businessman." *Bus Hist Rev*, XL (1966), 24-46.

11 PROWN, Jules D. "The Art Historian and the Computer; An Analysis of Copley's Patronage, 1753-1774." *Smithsonian J Hist*, I (1967), 17-30. See 65.10.

12 SCHLESINGER, Arthur M. "The Aristocracy in Colonial America." *Proc Mass Hist Soc*, LXXIV (1963), 3-21.

13 SHERIDAN, Richard B. "The Rise of a Colonial Gentry: A Case Study of Antigua, 1730-1775." *Econ Hist Rev*, 2d ser., XIII (1961), 342-357.

14 SHIPTON, Clifford K. "Ye Mystery of Ye Ages Solved, or, How Placing Worked at Colonial Harvard and Yale." *Har Alum Bull*, LVII (1954-1955), 258-259, 262-263 (cf. 417).

15 SHRYOCK, Richard H. *Medicine and Society in America, 1660-1860*. New York, 1960.†

16 SIRMANS, M. Eugene. "Politicians and Planters: The Bull Family of Colonial South Carolina." *Proc S C Hist Assn* (1962), 32-41.

17 SURRENCY, Erwin C. "The Lawyer and the Revolution." *Am J Leg Hist*, VIII (1964), 125-135.

18 SYDNOR, Charles S. *Gentlemen Freeholders; Political Practices in Washington's Virginia*. Chapel Hill, 1952.†

19 TOLLES, Frederick B. *Meeting House and Counting House: The Quaker Merchants of Colonial Philadelphia*. Chapel Hill, 1948.†

20 WALLACE, David D. *Life of Henry Laurens*. New York, 1915.

1 WARDEN, G. B. "The Proprietary Group in Pennsylvania, 1754-1764." *Wm Mar Q*, 3d ser., XXI (1964), 367-389.

2 WATERS, John J. *The Otis Family in Provincial and Revolutionary Massachusetts.* Chapel Hill, 1968.

3 WHITE, Philip L. *The Beckmans of New York in Politics and Commerce, 1647-1877.* . . . New York, 1956.

4 BAILYN, Bernard. "The Beekmans of New York: Trade, Politics, and Families." *Wm Mar Q*, 3d ser., XIV (1957), 601-602.

5 WRIGHT, Louis B. *The First Gentleman of Virginia; Intellectual Qualities of the Early Colonial Ruling Class.* San Marino, Calif., 1940.†

6 WROTH, Lawrence C. *The Colonial Printer.* New York, 1931.†

7 ZEMSKY, Robert M. "Power, Influence, and Status: Leadership Patterns in the Massachusetts Assembly." *Wm Mar Q*, 3d ser., XXVI (1969), 502-520.

B. AUTHORITY, DEMOCRACY, AND DEFERENCE

8 BAILYN, Bernard. *Origins of American Politics.* New York, 1968.†

9 BECKER, Carl L. *The History of Political Parties in the Province of New York, 1760-1776.* Madison, 1909; repr. 1960.†

10 BILLIAS, George A., ed. *Law and Authority in Colonial America: Selected Essays.* Barre, Mass., 1965.

11 BROWN, Robert E. *Middle-Class Democracy and the Revolution in Massachusetts, 1691-1780.* Ithaca, N.Y., 1955.†

12 BROWN, Robert E. and B. Katherine. *Virginia, 1705-1786: Democracy or Aristocracy?* East Lansing, Mich., 1964.

13 CARY, John. "Statistical Method and the Brown Thesis on Colonial Democracy." *Wm Mar Q*, 3d ser., XX (1963), 251-264. (See also Brown's reply, 265-276.)

14 BUEL, Richard, Jr. "Democracy and the American Revolution: A Frame of Reference." *Wm Mar Q*, 3d ser., XXI (1964), 165-190.

15 CECIL, Robert. "Oligarchy and Mob-Rule in the American Revolution." *Hist Today*, XIII (1963), 197-204.

16 COLEGROVE, Kenneth. "New England Town Mandates: Instructions to the Deputies in Colonial Legislatures." *Pub Col Soc Mass*, XXI (1920), 411-449.

17 DANIELL, Jere R. "Politics in New Hampshire Under Governor Benning Wentworth, 1741-1767." *Wm Mar Q*, 3d ser., XXIII (1966), 76-105.

18 FITZROY, Herbert W. K. "The Punishment of Crime in Provincial Pennsylvania." *Pa Mag Hist*, LX (1936), 242-269.

19 GIPSON, Lawrence H. "Crime and Its Punishment in Provincial Pennsylvania: A Phase of the Social History of the Commonwealth." *Pa Hist*, II (1935), 3-16.

1 GIPSON, Lawrence H. "The Criminal Codes of Connecticut." *J Am Inst Crim Law*, VI (1915), 177-189.

2 GOEBEL, Julius, Jr., and T. Raymond NAUGHTON. *Law Enforcement in Colonial New York; a Study in Criminal Procedure (1664-1776)*. New York, 1944.

3 GRANT, Charles S. *Democracy in the Connecticut Frontier Town of Kent.* New York, 1961.

4 GREENE, Jack P. "Changing Interpretations of Early American Politics." In *The Reinterpretation of Early American History*, ed. R. A. Billington. San Marino, Calif., 1966.†

5 GREENE, Jack P. "The Role of the Lower Houses of Assembly in Eighteenth-Century Politics." *J S Hist*, XXXVII (1961), 451-474.

6 KLEIN, Milton M. "Democracy and Politics in Colonial New York." *N Y Hist*, XL (1959), 221-246.

7 LEDER, Lawrence H. "The Role of Newspapers in Early America: 'In Defense of Their Own Liberty.'" *Hunt Lib Q*, XXX (1966), 1-16.

8 LOKKEN, Roy N. "The Concept of Democracy in Colonial Political Thought." *Wm Mar Q*, 3d ser., XVI (1959), 568-580.

9 LONGLEY, R. S. "Mob Activities in Revolutionary Massachusetts." *N Eng Q*, VI (1933), 98-130.

10 MC KINELY, Albert E. *The Suffrage Franchise in the Thirteen English Colonies in America.* Philadelphia, 1905.

11 MAIER, Pauline. "Popular Uprisings and Civil Authority in Eighteenth-Century America." *Wm Mar Q*, 3d ser., XXVII (1970), 3-35.

12 MORTON, Louis. "The Origins of American Military Policy." *Mil Affairs*, XXII (1958), 75-82.

13 MURRIN, John M. "The Myths of Colonial Democracy and Royal Decline in Eighteenth-Century America: A Review Essay." *Cithara*, V (1965), 53-69.

14 POLE, J. R. "Historians and the Problem of Early American Democracy." *Am Hist Rev*, LXVII (1962), 626-646.

15 RADABAUGH, Jack S. "The Militia as a Social Outlet in Colonial Massachusetts." *Soc Stud*, XLIX (1958), 106-109.

16 TAYLOR, Robert J. *Western Massachusetts in the American Revolution.* Providence, 1954.

17 THOMPSON, Mack F. "The Ward-Hopkins Controversy and the American Revolution in Rhode Island: An Interpretation." *Wm Mar Q*, 3d ser., XVI (1959), 363-375.

18 VARGA, Nicholas. "Election Procedures and Practices in Colonial New York." *N Y Hist*, 41 (July 1960), 249-277.

19 WOOD, Gordon S. "A Note on Mobs in the American Revolution." *Wm Mar Q*, 3d ser., XXIII (1966), 635-642.

1 ZUCKERMAN, Michael. *Peacable Kingdoms: New England Towns in the Eighteenth Century*. New York, 1970.

2 ZUCKERMAN, Michael. "The Social Context of Democracy in Massachusetts." *Wm Mar Q*, 3d ser., XXV (1968), 523-544.

C. OUTSIDERS: NEGROES, INDIANS, AND THE POOR

3 BENTON, Josiah H. *Warning Out in New England, 1656-1817*. Boston, 1911.

4 COLEMAN, Peter J. "The Insolvent Debtor in Rhode Island, 1745-1828." *Wm Mar Q*, 3d ser., XXII (1965), 413-434.

5 CORKRAN, David H. *The Cherokee Frontiers: Conflict and Survival, 1740-62*. Norman, Okla., 1962.

6 DAVIS, David B. *The Problem of Slavery in Western Culture*. Ithaca, N.Y., 1966.†

7 DEGLER, Carl N. "Slavery and the Genesis of American Race Prejudice." *Comp Stud Hist Soc*, II (1959), 49-66.

8 DOWNES, Randolph C. *Council Fires on the Upper Ohio: A Narrative of Indian Affairs in the Upper Ohio Valley Until 1795*. Pittsburgh, 1940.†

9 FEER, Robert A. "Imprisonment for Debt in Massachusetts Before 1800." *Miss Val Hist Rev*, XLVIII (1961), 252-269.

10 GOVEIA, Elsa V. *Slave Society in the British Leeward Islands at the End of the Eighteenth Century*. New Haven, 1965.

11 HANDLIN, Oscar and Mary. "The Origins of the Southern Labor System." *Wm Mar Q*, 3d ser., VII (1950), 199-222.

12 HAYWOOD, C. Robert. "Mercantilism and Colonial Slave Labor, 1700-1763." *J S Hist*, XXIII (1957), 454-469.

13 JENNINGS, Francis. "The Indian Trade of the Susquehanna Valley." *Proc Am Philos Soc*, CX (1966), 406-424.

14 JERNEGAN, Marcus W. "The Development of Poor Relief in Colonial Virginia." *Soc Ser Rev*, III (1929), 1-19.

15 JERNEGAN, Marcus W. "Slavery and Conversion in the American Colonies." *Am Hist Rev*, XXI (1916), 504-527.

16 JONES, Jerome W. "The Established Virginia Church and the Conversion of Negroes and Indians, 1620-1760." *J Neg Hist*, XLVL, (1961), 12-23.

17 JORDAN, Winthrop D. "Modern Tensions and the Origins of American Slavery." *J S Hist*, XXVII (1952), 18-33.

18 JORDON, Winthrop D. *White over Black: The Development of American Attitudes Toward the Negro, 1550-1812*. Chapel Hill, 1968.†

19 KELSO, Robert W. *History of Public Poor Relief in Massachusetts, 1620-1920*. Boston, 1922.

20 KLEIN, Herbert S. *Slavery in the Americas: A Comparative Study of Cuba and Virginia*. Chicago, 1967.

1   KLINGBERG, Frank J. *Anglican Humanitarianism in Colonial New York.* Philadelphia, 1940.

2   LAUBER, Almon W. *Indian Slavery in Colonial Times Within the Present Limits of the United States.* New York, 1913.

3   MILLING, Chapman J. *Red Carolinians.* Chapel Hill, 1940.

4   QUARLES, Benjamin. "The Colonial Militia and Negro Manpower." *Miss Val Hist Rev*, XLV (1958-1959), 634-652.

5   RANDALL, Edwin T. "Imprisonment for Debt in America: Fact and Fiction." *Miss Val Hist Rev*, XXXIX (1952), 89-102.

6   SIO, Arnold A. "Interpretations of Slavery: The Slave Status in the Americas." *Comp Stud Hist Soc*, VII (1965), 289-308.

7   SIRMANS, M. Eugene. "The Legal Status of the Slave in South Carolina, 1670-1740." *J S Hist*, XXVIII (1926), 462-473.

8   SMITH, Abbot E. *Colonists in Bondage: White Servitude and Convict Labor in America 1607-1776.* Chapel Hill, 1947.

9   WAX, Darold D. "The Demand for Slave Labor in Colonial Pennsylvania." *Pa Hist*, XXXIV (1967), 331-345.

10 WILLIS, William S. "Divide and Rule: Red, White, and Black in the Southeast." *J Neg Hist*, XLVIII (1963), 157-176.

11 YOUNG, Henry J. "A Note on Scalp Bounties in Pennsylvania." *Pa Hist*, XXIV (1957), 207-218.

4. The Economy

A. AGRICULTURE

12 *American Husbandry 1775*, ed. Harry J. Carman. New York, 1939.

13 BEAN, Walton E. "War and the British Colonial Farmer: A Re-evaluation in the Light of New Statistical Records." *Pac Hist Rev*, XI (1942), 439-447.

14 EISINGER, Chester E. "The Farmer in the Eighteenth-Century Almanac." *Ag Hist*, XXVIII (1954), 107-112.

15 GRAY, Lewis C. *History of Agriculture in the Southern United States to 1860.* 2 vols. Washington, D.C. 1933.

16 KLINGARNAN, David. "The Significance of Grain in the Development of the Tobacco Colonies." *J Econ Hist*, XXIX (1969), 268-278.

17 LAND, Aubrey C. "Economic Behavior in a Planting Society: The Eighteenth-Century Chesapeake." *J S Hist*, XXXIII (1967), 469-585.

18 LEMON, James T. "The Agricultural Practices of National Groups in Eighteenth-Century Southeastern Pennsylvania." *Geog Rev*, LVI (1966), 467-496.

19 LOEHR, Rodney C. "Self-Sufficiency on the Farm." *Ag Hist*, XXVI (1952), 37-42.

1 POTTER, David M., Jr. "The Rise of the Plantation System in Georgia." *Ga Hist Q*, XVI (1932), 114-135.

SACHS, William S. "Agricultural Conditions in the Northern Colonies Before the Revolution." *J Econ Hist*, XIII (1953), 274-290.

3 SCHLEBECKER, John T., ed. "Eighteenth-Century Agriculture: A Symposium." *Ag Hist*, XLIII (1969), 1-186.

4 SHRYOCK, Richard H. "British Versus German Traditions in Colonial Agriculture." *Miss Val Hist Rev*, XXVI (1939), 39-54.

5 WALCOTT, Robert. "Husbandry in Colonial New England." *N Eng Q*, IX (1936), 218-252.

B. COMMERCE AND MONEY

6 BROCK, Leslie V. "The Currency of the American Colonies, 1700-1764: A Study in Colonial Finance and Imperial Relations." Unpublished Ph. D. thesis, U. of Michigan, 1941.

7 BRUCHEY, Stuary. *The Roots of American Economic Growth, 1607-1861: An Essay in Social Causation.* London and New York, 1965.†

8 BRUCHEY, Stuart. "Success and Failure Factors: American Merchants in Foreign Trade in the Eighteenth and Early Nineteenth Centuries." *Bus Hist Rev*, XXXII (1958), 272-292.

9 BURSTEIN, M. L. "Colonial Currency and Contemporary Monetary Theory: A Review Article." *Explor Entrep Hist* 2d ser., III (1966), 220-233.

10 COLE, Arthur H. "The Tempo of Mercantile Life in Colonial America." *Bus Hist Rev*, XXXIII (1959), 277-299.

11 EDELMAN, Edward. "Thomas Hancock, Colonial Merchant." *J Econ Bus Hist*, I (1928), 77-104.

12 FERGUSON, E. James. "Currency Finance: An Interpretation of Colonial Monetary Practices." *Wm Mar Q*, 3d ser., X (1953), 153-180.

13 GRAY, Lewis C. "The Market Surplus Problem of Colonial Tobacco." *Ag Hist*, II (1928), 1-34.

14 HARRINGTON, Virginia D. *The New York Merchant on the Eve of the Revolution.* New York, 1935.

15 HIGGINS, W. Robert. "Charles Town Merchants and Factors Dealing in the External Negro Trade, 1735-1775." *S C Hist Mag*, LXV (1964), 205-217.

16 JELLISON, Richard M. "Paper Currency in Colonial South Carolina: A Reappraisal." *S C Hist Mag* LXII (1961), 134-147.

17 JENSEN, Arthur L. *The Maritime Commerce of Colonial Philadelphia.* Madison, 1963.

18 LESTER, Richard A. *Monetary Experiments, Early American and Recent Scandinavian.* Princeton, 1939.

1 LYDON, James G. "Fish and Flour for Gold: Southern Europe and the Colonial American Balance of Payments." *Bus Hist Rev*, XXXIX (1965), 171-183.

2 MARTIN, Margaret E. "Merchants and Trade of the Connecticut River Valley, 1750-1820." *Stud Hist* (Smith), XXIV (1939), 1-284.

3 MORISON, Samuel E. "The Commerce of Boston on the Eve of the Revolution." *Proc Am Ant Soc*, n.s. XXXII (1923), 24-51.

4 OSTRANDER, Milman M. "The Colonial Molasses Trade." *Ag Hist*, XXX (1956), 77-84.

5 PARES, Richard. *Merchants and Planters*. New York, 1960.†

6 PARES, Richard. *Yankees and Creoles. The Trade Between North America and the West Indies Before the American Revolution*. London, 1956.

7 PRICE, Jacob M. "The Economic Growth of the Chesapeake and the European Market, 1697-1775." *J Econ Hist*, XXIV (1964), 496-511.

8 PRICE, Jacob M. "The Rise of Glasgow in the Chesapeake Tobacco Trade, 1707-1775." *Wm Mar Q*, 3d ser., XI (1954), 179-199.

9 SAUL, Norman E. "The Beginnings of American-Russian Trade, 1763-1766." *Wm Mar Q*, 3d ser., XXVI (1969), 596-600.

10 SELLERS, Leila. *Charleston Business on the Eve of the Revolution*. Chapel Hill, 1934.

11 SHEPHERD, James F. "A Balance of Payments for the Thirteen Colonies, 1768-1772: A Summary." *J Econ Hist*, XXV (1965), 691-695.

12 SHEPHERD, James F., and Gary M. WALTON. "Estimates of 'Invisible' Earnings in the Balance of Payments of the British North America Colonies, 1768-1772." *J Econ Hist*, XXIX (1969), 230-263.

13 SHERIDAN, Richard B. "The Molasses Act and the Market Strategy of the British Sugar Planters." *J Econ Hist*, XVII (1957), 62-83.

14 THAYER, Theodore G. "The Land-Bank System in the American Colonies." *J Econ Hist*, XIII (1953), 145-159.

15 THOMSON, Robert P. "The Tobacco Export of the Upper James River Naval District, 1773-75." *Wm Mar Q*, 3d ser., XVIII (1961), 393-407.

16 WALTON, Gary M. "Sources of Productivity Change in American Colonial Shipping, 1675-1775." *Econ Hist Rev*, 2d ser., XX (1967), 67-78.

17 WAX, Donald D. "Quaker Merchants and the Slave Trade in Colonial Pennsylvania." *Pa Mag Hist*, LXXXVI (1962), 143-159.

C. MANUFACTURING

18 BINING, Arthur C. "The Iron Plantations of Early Pennsylvania." *Pa Mag Hist*, LVII (1933), 117-137.

1 CLARK, Victor S. *History of Manufacturers in the United States.* 3 vols. New York, 1929.

2 HAMER, Marguerite B. "The Foundation and Failure of the Silk Industry in Provincial Georgia." *N C Hist Rev*, XII (1935), 125-148.

3 HAYWOOD, C. Robert. "Economic Sanctions: Use of the Threat of Manufacturing by the Southern Colonies." *J S Hist*, XXV (1959), 207-219.

4 JERNEGAN, Marcus W. "Slavery and the Beginning of Industrialism in the American Colonies." *Am Hist Rev*, XXV (1920), 220-240.

5 WELSH, Peter C. "The Brandywine Mills: A Chronicle of an Industry, 1762-1816." *Del Hist*, VII (1956), 17-36.

6 WELSH, Peter C. "Merchants, Millers and Ocean Ships: The Components of an Early American Industrial Town." *Del Hist*, VII (1957), 319-336.

D. PRICES, WAGES, INCOME, AND WEALTH

7 BEZANSON, Anne, Robert D. GRAY, and Miriam HUSSEY. *Prices in Colonial Pennsylvania.* Philadelphia, 1935.

8 Bureau of Labor Statistics. *Wages in the Colonial Period.* (Bulletin 499.) Washington, D.C., 1929.

9 COLE, Arthur H. *Wholesale Commodity Prices in the United States, 1700-18.* Cambridge, Mass., 1938.

10 EVANS, Emory. "Planter Indebtedness and the Coming of the Revolution in Virginia." *Wm Mar Q*, 3d ser., XIX (1962), 511-533.

11 GIPSON, Lawrence H. "Virginia Planter Debts Before the American Revolution." *Va Mag Hist*, LXIX (1961), 259-277.

12 JONES, Alice Hanson. "Wealth Estimates for the American Middle Colonies, 1774." *Economic Development and Cultural Change*, XVIII (1970), 1-172.

13 LEMON, James T. "Household Consumption in Eighteenth-Century America and Its Relationship to Production and Trade: The Situation Among Farmers in Southeastern Pennsylvania." *Ag Hist*, XLI (1967), 67-70.

14 TAYLOR, George R. "Wholesale Commodity Prices at Charleston, South Carolina, 1732-1791." *J Econ Bus Hist*, IV (1932), 356-377.

15 TOLLES, Frederick B. "Town House and Country House Inventories from the Estate of William Logan, 1776." *Pa Mag Hist*, LXXXII (1958), 397-410.

5. Culture, Values, and Outlook

A. RELIGION AND CHURCHES

1 BURR, Nelson R., with J. W. SMITH, and A. L. JAMISON, eds. *A Critical Bibliography of Religion in America.* 2 vols. Princeton, 1961.

2 BALDWIN, Alice M. *The New England Clergy and the American Revolution.* Durham, N.C., 1928.

3 BALDWIN, Alice M. "Sowers of Sedition: The Political Theories of Some of the New Light Presbyterian Clergy of Virginia and North Carolina." *Wm Mar Q*, 3d ser., V (1948), 52-76.

4 BRYDON, George M. *Virginia's Mother Church and the Political Conditions Under Which It Grew: The Story of the Anglican Church and the Development of Religion in Virginia, 1727-1814.* Philadelphia, 1952.

5 BUMSTED, J. M. "Revivalism and Separatism in New England: The First Society of Norwich, Connecticut, as a Case Study." *Wm Mar Q*, 3d ser., XXIV (1967), 588-612.

6 CONKIN, Paul. "The Church Establishment in North Carolina, 1765-1776." *N C Hist Rev*, XXXII (1955), 1-30.

7 DAVIDSON, Elizabeth. *The Establishment of the English Church in Continental American Colonies.* Durham, N.C., 1936.

8 ELLIS, John T. *Catholics in Colonial America.* Baltimore, 1965.

9 ERVIN, Spencer. "The Establishment, Government, and Functioning of the Church in Colonial Virginia." *Hist Mag P E Ch*, XXVI (1957), 65-110.

10 GAUSTAD, Edwin S. *The Great Awakening in New England.* New York, 1957.†

11 GOEN, C. C. *Revivalism and Separatism in New England, 1740-1800: Strict Congregationalists and Separate Baptists in the Great Awakening.* New Haven, 1962.

12 HANLEY, Thomas O. "Colonial Protestantism and the Rise of Democracy." *Am Ecc Rev*, CXLI (1959), 24-32.

13 HEIMERT, Alan. *Religion and the American Mind from the Great Awakening to the Revolution.* Cambridge, Mass., 1966.

14 MC LOUGHLIN, William G. "The American Revolution as a Religious Revival: The Millenium in One Country." *N Eng Q*, XL (1967), 99-110. (Review of Heimert.)

15 JAMES, Sydney V. *A People Among Peoples: Quaker Benevolence in Eighteenth-Century America.* Cambridge, Mass., 1963.

1 KRAMER, Leonard J. "Presbyterians Approach the American Revolution." *J Presby Hist Soc*, XXXI (1953), 71-86, 167-180.

2 MC LOUGHLIN, William G. "The First Calvinistic Baptist Association in New England, 1754-1767." *C Hist*, XXXVI (1967), 410-418.

3 MC LOUGHLIN, William G. *Isaac Backus and the American Pietistic Tradition.* Boston, 1967.

4 MAXSON, Charles H. *The Great Awakening in the Middle Colonies.* Chicago, 1920.

5 MEAD, Sidney E. "From Coercion to Persuasion. Another Look at the Rise of Religious Liberty and the Emergence of Denominationalism (1607-1791)." *C Hist*, XXV (1956), 317-337.

6 MEAD, Sidney E. "The Rise of the Evangelical Conception of the Ministry in America: 1607-1850." In *The Ministry in Historical Perspective*, ed. Richard Niebuhr and others. New York, 1956.

7 MILLER, Perry. "From the Covenant to the Revival." In *Shaping of American Religion.* Vol I. of *Religion in American Life*, eds. J. W. Smith and A. L. Jamison. Princeton, 1961.

8 MORAIS, Herbert M. *Deism in Eighteenth-Century America. Stud Hist Econ Pub Law* (Colum), No. 397. London and New York, 1934.

9 MORGAN, Davie T., Jr. "The Great Awakening in North Carolina, 1740-1775: The Baptist Phase." *N C Hist Rev*, XLV (1968), 264-283.

10 MORGAN, Edmund S. "The Puritan Ethic and the American Revolution." *Wm Mar Q*, 3d ser., XXIV, 3-43.

11 SCOTT, Robert F. "Colonial Presbyterianism in the Valley of Virginia, 1727-1775." *J Presby Hist Soc*, XXV (1957), 71-92, 171-192.

12 SEILER, William H. "The Anglican Parish Vestry in Colonial Virginia." *J S Hist*, XXII (1956), 310-337.

13 SKLAR, Robert. "The Great Awakening and Colonial Politics: Connecticut's Revolution in the Minds of Men." *Bull Conn Hist Soc*, XXVIII (1963), 81-95.

14 TUCKER, Louis L. "The Church of England and Religious Liberty at Pre-Revolutionary Yale." *Wm Mar Q*, XVII (1960), 314-328.

15 VAN TYNE, Claude H. "Influence of the Clergy, and of Religious and Sectarian Forces on the American Revolution." *Am Hist Rev*, XIX (1913), 44-64.

16 WINSLOW, Ola E. *Meetinghouse Hill, 1630-1783.* New York, 1952.

B. EDUCATION AND INTELLECTUAL LIFE

17 BAILYN, Bernard. *Education in the Forming of American Society: Needs and Opportunities for Study.* Chapel Hill, 1960.†

1   BELL, Whitfield J. *Early American Science: Needs and Opportunities for Study.* Williamsburg, 1955.

2   WHITEHILL, Walter M. *The Arts in Early American History.* Chapel Hill, 1965.

3   BRODERICK, Francis L. "Pulpit, Physics, and Politics: The Curriculum of the College of New Jersey, 1746-1794." *Wm Mar Q,* 3d ser., VI (1949), 42-68.

4   BRONSON, Walter C. *The History of Brown University, 1764-1914.* Providence, 1914.

5   CHEYNEY, Edward P. *History of the University of Pennsylvania, 1740-1940.* Philadelphia, 1940.

6   COME, Donald R. "The Influence of Princeton on Higher Education in the South Before 1825." *Wm Mar Q,* 3d ser., II (1945), 352-396.

7   GUMMERE, Richard M. *The American Colonial Mind and the Classical Tradition: Essays in Comparative Culture.* Cambridge, Mass., 1963.

8   HINDLE, Brooke. *The Pursuit of Science in Revolutionary America, 1735-1789.* Chapel Hill, 1956.†

9   JERNEGAN, Marcus W. "The Educational Development of the Southern Colonies." *School Rev,* XXVII (1919), 360-376, 405-425.

10 JONES, Howard M. *America and French Culture, 1750-1848.* Chapel Hill, 1927.

11 JONES, Howard M. "American Prose Style: 1700-1770." *Hunt Lib Bull,* No. 6 (1934), 115-151.

12 KRAUS, Michael. *The Atlantic Civilization: Eighteenth-Century Origins.* Ithaca, N.Y., 1949.

13 MC ANEAR, Beverly. "College Founding in the American Colonies, 1745-1775." *Miss Val Hist Rev,* XLII (1955), 24-44.

14 MC CALLUM, James D. *Eleazar Wheelock: The Founder of Dartmouth College.* Hanover, N.H., 1939.

15 MC CAUL, Robert L. "Education in Georgia During the Period of Royal Government, 1752-1776 . . . ." *Ga Hist Q,* XL (1956), 103-112, 248-259.

16 MC KEEHAN, Louis W. *Yale Science: The First Hundred Years, 1701-1801.* New York, 1947.

7   MIDDLEKAUF, Robert. *Ancients and Axioms: Secondary Education in Eighteenth-Century New England.* New Haven, 1963.

18 MORISON, Samuel E. *Three Centuries of Harvard, 1636-1936.* Cambridge, Mass., 1936.

19 PARRINGTON, Vernon L. *Main Currents in American Thought; An Interpretation of American Literature from the Beginning to 1920.* 3 vols., 1927-1930. Vol. I: *The Colonial Mind.* New York, 1927.†

1 SCHMIDT, George P. *Princeton and Rutgers: The Two Colonial College of New Jersey.* Princeton, 1964.

2 SEYBOLT, Robert F. *The Public Schools of Colonial Boston, 1635-1775.* Cambridge, Mass., 1935.

3 SPURLIN, Paul M. *Montesquieu in America, 1760-1801.* Baton Rouge, 1940.

4 SPURLIN, Paul M. *Rousseau in America, 1760-1809.* University, Ala., 1969.

5 TUCKER, Louis L. *Puritan Protagonist: President Thomas Clap of Yale College.* Chapel Hill, 1962.

6 TYLER, Lyon G. *The College of William and Mary in Virginia: Its History and Work, 1693-1907.* Richmond, Va., 1907.

7 WERTENBAKER, Thomas J. *Princeton, 1746-1896.* Princeton, 1946.

8 WRIGHT, Louis B. "Intellectual History and the Colonial South." *Wm Mar Q*, 3d ser., XVI (1959), 214-227.

C. ATTITUDES AND BELIEF

9 BAILYN, Bernard. *Ideological Origins of the American Revolution.* Cambridge, Mass., 1967.

10 BAILYN, Bernard. "Political Experience and Enlightenment Ideas in Eighteenth-Century America." *Am Hist Rev*, LXVII (1962), 339-351.

11 BARKER, Charles A. "Maryland Before the Revolution: Society and Thought." *Am Hist Rev*, XLVI (1940), 1-20.

12 BOORSTIN, Daniel. *The Americans; The Colonial Experience.* New York, 1958.†

13 BROCK, Peter. *Pacifism in the United States from the Colonial Era to the First World War.* Princeton, 1968.

14 BROOKES, George S. *Friend Anthony Benezet.* London and Philadelphia, 1937.

15 COLBOURN, H. Trevor. *The Lamp of Experience: Whig History and the Intellectual Origins of the American Revolution.* Chapel Hill, 1965.

16 DIAMOND, Sigmund. "Values as an Obstacle to Economic Growth: The American Colonies." *J Econ Hist*, XXVII, No. 4 (1967), 561-575.

17 GREENE, Evarts B. "The Code of Honor in Colonial and Revolutionary Times, with Special Reference to New England." *Pub Col Soc Mass*, XXVI (1927), 367-388.

18 GREENE, Jack P., ed. *The Diary of Colonel Landon Carter of Sabine Hall, 1752-1778.* 2 vols. Charlottesville, Va., 1965.

19 HOYT, Edward A. "Naturalization Under the American Colonies: Signs of a New Community." *Pol Sci Q*, LXVII (1938), 70-79.

1 KELLER, Hans Gustav. *Die Wurzeln der Amerikanischen Demokratie.* Bern, 1956.

2 KOCH, Adrienne. "Pragmatic Wisdom and the American Enlightenment." *Wm Mar Q*, 3d ser., XVIII (1961), 313-329.

3 LITTO, Fredric M. "Affison's Cato in the Colonies." *Wm Mar Q*, 3d ser., XXIII (1966), 431-449.

4 LUDWIG, Allen I. *Graven Images: New England Stonecarving and Its Symbols, 1650-1815.* Middletown, Conn., 1966.

5 MULLETT, Charles F. "Classical Influences on the American Revolution." *Clas J*, XXXV (1939-1940), 92-104.

6 PERSONS, Stow. "The Cyclical Theory of History in Eighteenth-Century America." *Am Q*, VI (1954), 147-163.

7 ROBBINS, Caroline. "'When It Is That Colonies May Turn Independent': An Analysis of the Enviornment and Politics of Francis Hutcheson (1699-1746)." *Wm Mar Q*, 3d ser., XI (1954), 214-251.

8 ROSSITER, Clinton. *Seedtime of the Republic; The Origins of the American Tradition of Political Liberty.* New York, 1953.†

9 SAVELLE, Max. *Seeds of Liberty: The Genesis of the American Mind.* New York, 1948.†

10 WOODWARD, C. Vann. "The Southern Ethic in a Puritan World." *Wm Mar Q*, XXV (1968), 343-370.

6. Conflict, Mobility, and Change

11 ABERNETHY, Thomas P. *Three Virginia Frontiers.* Baton Rouge, 1940.

12 AKAGI, Roy H. *The Town Proprietors of the New England Colonies: A Study of Their Development, Organization, Activities and Controversies, 1620-1770.* Philadelphia, 1924.

13 BAILEY, Edith A. "Influences Toward Radicalism in Connecticut, 1754-1775." *Stud Hist* (Smith), V (1919-1920), 175-252.

14 BASSETT, John S. "The Regulators of North Carolina, 1765-1771." *Ann Rep Am Hist Assn for the Year 1894.* Washington, D.C., 1895, pp. 141-212.

15 BILLIAS, George A. "Pox and Politics in Marblehead, 1773-4." *Essex Inst Hist Coll*, XCLL (1956), 43-58.

16 BOYD, Julian P. *The Susquehannah Company: Connecticut's Experiment in Expansion.* New Haven, 1935.

17 BRENNAN, Ellen E. *Plural Office-Holding in Massachusetts, 1760-1780: Its Relation to the "Separation" of Departments of Government.* Chapel Hill, 1945.

18 BRIDENBAUGH, Carl. "Violence and Virtue in Virginia, 1766." *Proc Mass Hist Soc*, LXXVI (1964), 3-29.

•

1 BROWN, Richard M. *The South Carolina Regulators.* Cambridge, Mass., 1963.

2 BUSHMAN, Richard L. *From Puritan to Yankee: Character and the Social Order in Connecticut, 1690-1765.* Cambridge, Mass., 1967.†

3 CAMPBELL, Mildred. "English Emigration on the Eve of the American Revolution." *Am Hist Rev*, LXI (1955), 1-20.

4 COOK, Edward M. Jr. "Social Behaviour and Changing Values in Dedham, Massachusetts, 1700 to 1775." *Wm Mar Q*, 3d ser., XXVII (1970), 546-80.

5 CRARY, Catherine S. "The American Dream: John Tabor Kempe's Rise from Poverty to Riches." *Wm Mar Q*, 3d ser., XIV (1957), 176-195.

6 CRARY, Catherine S. "The Humble Immigrant and the American Dream: Some Case Histories, 1746-1776." *Miss Val Hist Rev*, XLVI (1959), 46-66.

7 CUMMINGS, Hubertis M. "The Paxton Killings." *J Presby Hist Soc*, XLIV (1966), 291-243.

8 DAVIDSON, Philip G. "The Southern Backcountry on the Eve of the Revolution." In *Essays in Honor of William E. Dodd*, ed. Avery Craven. Chicago, 1935.

9 DICKSON, R. J. *Ulster Emigration to Colonial America, 1718-1775.* New York, 1966.

10 DIFFENDERFFER, Frank R. *The German Immigration into Pennsylvania Through the Port of Philadelphia from 1700 to 1775.* Lancaster, Pa., 1900.

11 DODDRIDGE, Joseph. *Notes on the Settlement and Indian Wars of the Western Parts of Virginia and Pennsylvania, 1763-83 . . . .* Wellsburgh, Va., 1824; Albany, 1876.

12 FOX, Dixon R. *Yankees and Yorkers.* New York, 1940.

13 FRANKLIN, W. Neil. "Pennsylvania-Virginia Rivalry for the Indian Trade of the Ohio Valley." *Miss Val Hist Rev*, XX (1934), 463-480.

14 GIDDENS, Paul H. "Land Policies and Administration in Colonial Maryland, 1753-1769." *Md Hist Mag*, XXVIII (1933), 142-171.

15 GRAHAM, Ian C. C. *Colonists from Scotland. Emigration to North America, 1707-1783.* Ithaca, N.Y., 1956.

16 GREEN, E. R. R. "Queensborough Township: Scotch-Irish Emigration and the Expansion of Georgia, 1763-1776." *Wm Mar Q*, 3d ser., XVII (1960), 183-199.

17 GREEN, E. R. R. "The Scotch-Irish and the Coming of the Revolution in North Carolina." *Irish Hist Stud*, VII (1950), 77-86.

18 GREENE, Jack P. *The Quest for Power: The Lower Houses of Assembly in the Southern Royal Colonies, 1689-1776.* Chapel Hill, 1963.

1 HANDLIN, Oscar. "The Eastern Frontier of New York." *N Y Hist*, XVIII (1937), 50-75.

2 HANSEN, Marcus L. *The Atlantic Migration, 1607-1860: A History of the Continuing Settlement of the United States.* Cambridge, Mass., 1940.†

3 HENRETTA, James A. "Economic Development and Social Structure in Colonial Boston." *Wm Mar Q*, 3d ser., XXII (1965), 75-92.

4 HIGGINS, Ruth L. *Expansion in New York, with Especial Reference to the Eighteenth Century.* Columbus, Ohio, 1931.

5 HINDLE, Brooke. "The March of the Paxton Boys." *Wm Mar Q*, 3d ser., III (1946), 461-486.

6 HOOKER, Richard J., ed. *The Carolina Backcountry on the Eve of the Revolution: The Journal and Other Writings of Charles Woodmason, Anglican Itinerant.* Chapel Hill, 1953.

7 HUDSON, Arthur P. "Songs of the North Carolina Regulators." *Wm Mar Q*, 3d ser., IV (1947), 470-485.

8 JORDAN, John W. "Moravian Immigration to Pennsylvania, 1734-1765." *Pa Mag Hist*, XXXIII (1909), 228-248.

9 LEMON, James T., and Gary B. NASH. "The Distribution of Wealth in Eighteenth-Century America: A Century of Changes in Chester County, Pennsylvania, 1693-1802." *J Soc Hist*, II (1968), 1-24.

10 LEYBURN, James. *The Soctch-Irish: A Social History.* Chapel Hill, 1962.

11 LOCKRIDGE, Kenneth. "Land, Population and the Evolution of New England Society 1630-1790." *Past Pres*, No. 39 (1968), 62-80.

12 MARK, Irving. *Agrarian Conflicts in Colonial New York, 1711-1775.* New York, 1940.

13 MELLOR, George R. "Emigration from the Britisb Isles to the New World, 1765-1775." *History*, n.s. XL (1955), 68-83.

14 MERIWETHER, Robert L. *The Expansion of South Carolina, 1729-1765.* Kingsport, Tenn., 1940.

15 MEYER, Duane. *The Highland Scots of North Carolina, 1732-1776.* Chapel Hill, 1961.

16 MILLER, John C. "Religion, Finance, and Democracy in Massachusetts." *N Eng Q*, VI (1933), 19-58.

17 POLLAK, Otto. "German Immigrant Problems in Eighteenth-Century Pennsylvania as Reflected in Trouble Advertisements." *Am Soc Rev*, VIII (1943), 674-684.

18 POTTER, John E. "The Pennsylvania and Virginia Boundary Controversy." *Pa Mag Hist*, XXXVIII (1914), 407-426.

19 RAMSEY, Robert. *Carolina Cradle: Settlement of the Northwest Carolina Frontier, 1747-1762.* Chapel Hill, 1964.

20 ROTHERMUND, Dietmar. "The German Problem of Colonial Pennsylvania" *Pa Mag Hist*, LXXXIV (1960), 3-21.

1 SHY, John W. "A New Look at Colonial Militia." *Wm Mar Q*, 3d ser., XX (1963), 175-185.

2 SKAGGS, David C. "Maryland's Impulse Toward Social Revolution, 1750-1776." *J Am Hist*, LIV (1968), 771-786.

3 TILLEY, Nannie M. "Political Disturbances in Colonial Granville County." *N C Hist Rev*, XVIII (1941), 339-359.

4 WEAVER, Glenn. "Anglican-Congregationalist Tensions in Pre-Revolutionary Connecticut." *Hist Mag P E Ch*, XXVI (1957), 169-285.

5 WUST, Klaus. *The Virginia Germans.* Charlottesville, Va., 1969.

7. Intercolonial Relations

6 BLASSINGAME, John W. "American Nationalism and Other Loyalties in the Southern Colonies, 1763-1775." *J S Hist*, XXXIV (1968), 50-75.

7 BRIDENBAUGH, Carl. "Charlestonians at Newport, 1767-1775." *S C Hist Mag*, XLI (1940), 43-7.

8 CRAWFORD, Walter F. "The Commerce of Rhode Island with the Southern Continental Colonies in the Eighteenth Century." *R I Hist Soc Coll*, XIV (1921), 99-110, 124-130.

9 GIPSON, Lawrence H. "The Drafting of the Albany Plan of Union: A Problem in Semantics." *Pa Hist*, XXVI (1959), 291-316.

10 GIPSON, Lawrence H. "Massachusetts Bay and American Colonial Union, 1754." *Proc Am Ant Soc*, LXXI (1961), 63-92.

11 GIPSON, Lawrence H. "Thomas Hutchinson and the Framing of the Albany Plan of Union, 1754." *Pa Mag Hist*, LXXIV (1959), 5-35.

12 GREENE, Jack P. "Martin Bladen's Blueprint for a Colonial Union." *Wm Mar Q*, 3d ser., XVII (1960), 516-530.

13 HARKNESS, Albert, Jr. "Americanism and Jenkins' Ear." *Miss Val Hist Rev*, XXXVII (1950), 61-90.

14 KRAUS, Michael. *Intercolonial Aspects of American Culture on the Eve of the Revolution, with Special Reference to the Northern Towns.* New York, 1928.

15 MATHEWS, Lois K. "Benjamin Franklin's Plans for a Colonial Union, 1750-1775." *Am Pol Sci Rev*, VIII (1914), 393-412.

16 MERRITT, Richard L. *Symbols of American Community, 1735-1775.* New Haven, 1966.

17 MILLER, Ralph N. "American Nationalism as a Theory of Nature." *Wm Mar Q*, 3d ser., XII (1955), 64-95.

18 PECKHAM, Howard H. "Speculations on the Colonial Wars." *Wm Mar Q*, 3d ser., XVII (1960), 463-472.

19 SACHS, William S. "Interurban Correspondents and the Development of a National Economy before the Revolution: New York as a Case Study." *N Y Hist*, XXXVI (1955), 320-335.

1   SAVELLE, Max. "The Appearance of an American Attitude Toward External Affairs, 1750-1775." *Am Hist Rev*, LII (1947), 655-666.

2   SAVELLE, Max. "Nationalism and Other Loyalties in the American Revolution." *Am Hist Rev*, LXVII (1963), 901-923.

3   VARG, Paul A. "The Advent of Nationalism, 1758-1776." *Am Q*, XVI (1964), 169-182.

4   WHITSON, Agnes M. "The Outlook of the Continental American Colonies on the British West Indies, 1760-1775." *Pol Sci Q*, XLV (1930), 56-86.

IV. Empire and Imperial Reform

1. The Structure of the Empire

A. IMPERIAL ORGANIZATION

5   ANDREWS, Charles M. "The Royal Disallowance." *Proc Am Ant Soc*, XXIV (1914), 342-362.

6   BARROW, Thomas C. *Trade and Empire: The British Customs Service in Colonial America 1660-1775.* Cambridge, Mass., 1967.

7   BAYSE, Arthur H. *The Lords Commissioners of Trade and Plantations, Commonly Known as the Board of Trade, 1748-1782.* New Haven, 1925.

8   BOND, Beverly W. "The Colonial Agency as a Popular Representative." *Pol Sci Q*, XXXV (1920), 372-392.

9   BURNS, James J. *The Colonial Agents of New England.* Washington, D.C., 1935.

10 CLARK, Dora Mae. *The Rise of the British Treasure: Colonial Administration in the Eighteenth Century.* New Haven, 1960.

11 CLARKE, Mary Patterson. "The Board of Trade at Work." *Am Hist Rev*, XVII (1911), 17-43.

12 DICKERSON, Oliver M. *American Colonial Government 1696-1765: A Study of the British Board of Trade in Its Relation to the American Colonies, Political, Industrial, Administrative.* Cleveland, 1912.

13 ELLIS, Kenneth L. "British Communications and Diplomacy in the Eighteenth Century." *Bull Inst Hist Res*, XXXI (1958), 159-167.

14 LABAREE, Leonard W. *Royal Government in America, A Study of the British Colonial System Before 1783.* New Haven, 1930.

15 LABAREE, Leonard W., ed. *Royal Instructions to British Colonial Governors, 1670-1776.* 2 vols. London and New York, 1935.

1   LILY, Edward P. *The Colonial Agents of New York and New Jersey.* Washington, D.C., 1936.

2   LONN, Ella. *The Colonial Agents of the Southern Colonies.* Chapel Hill, 1945.

3   MC ANEAR, Beverly. *The Income of the Colonial Governors of British North America.* New York, 1967.

4   MORTON, W. L. "The Local Executive in the British Empire, 1763-1828." *Eng Hist Rev,* LXXVIII (1963), 436-457.

5   PENSON, Lilian M. *The Colonial Agents of the British West Indies: A Study in Colonial Administration, Mainly in the Eighteenth Century.* London, 1924.

6   SMITH, Joseph H. *Appeals to the Privy Council from the American Plantations.* New York, 1950.

7   THOMSON, Mark A. *The Secretaries of State, 1681-1782.* Oxford, 1932.

8   TURNER, Edward R. *The Privy Council of England in the Seventeenth and Eighteenth Centuries, 1603-1784.* 2 vols. Baltimore, 1927-1928.

9   WASHBURNE, George A. *Imperial Control of the Administration of Justice in the Thirteen Colonies, 1684-1776.* New York, 1923.

10   WICKWIRE, Franklin B. *British Subministers and Colonial America, 1763-1783.* Princeton, 1966.

11   WILKINSON, Norman B. "The Colonial Voice in London." *Historian,* III (1940), 22-36.

B. ECONOMIC ASPECTS

12   ASHTON, T. S. *Economic Fluctuations in England, 1700-1800.* Oxford, 1959.

13   ASHTON, T. S. *An Economic History of England: The Eighteenth Century.* New York, 1955.

14   BARKER, T. C. "Smuggling in the Eighteenth Century: The Evidence of the Scottish Tobacco Trade." *Va Mag Hist,* LXII (1954), 387-399.

15   CARTER, Alice. "Analysis of Public Indebtedness in Eighteenth-Century England." *Bull Inst Hist Res,* XXIV (1951), 173-181.

16   COLE, W. A. "Trends in Eighteenth-Century Smuggling." *Econ Hist Rev,* 2d ser., X (1958), 395-410.

17   DAVIS, Ralph. *A Commercial Revolution: English Overseas Trade in the Seventeenth and Eighteenth Centuries.* London, 1967.†

18   DAVIS, Ralph. *The Rise of the English Shipping Industry in the Seventeenth and Eighteenth Centuries.* New York, 1962.

19   DEANE, Phyllis, and W. A. COLE. *British Economic Growth, 1688-1959: Trends and Structure.* New York, 1967.

1 FARNIE, D. A. "The Commercial Empire of the Atlantic, 1607-1783." *Econ Hist Rev*, 2d ser., XV (1962), 105-218.

2 GOULD, J. D. "Agricultural Fluctuations and the English Economy in the Eighteenth Century." *J Econ Hist*, XXII (1962), 313-333.

3 HOH-CHENG, and Lorna H. MUI. "Smuggling and the British Tea Trade Before 1784." *Am Hist Rev*, LXXIV (1968), 44-73.

4 JAMES, Francis G. "Irish Colonial Trade in the Eighteenth Century." *Wm Mar Q*, 3d ser., XX (1963), 574-585.

5 LAWSON, Murray G. *Fur: A Study in English Mercantilism, 1700-1775*. Toronto, 1943.

6 NETTELS, Curtis P. "British Mercantilism and the Economic Development of the Thirteen Colonies." *J Econ Hist*, XII (1952), 105-114.

7 PARES, Richard. "The London Sugar Market, 1740-1769." *Econ Hist Rev*, 2d ser., IX (1956), 254-270.

8 PELHAM, R. A. "The West Midland Iron Industry and the American Market in the Eighteenth Century." *U Birmingham Hist J*, II (1950), 141-162.

9 PRICE, Jacob M. "Who Was John Norton? A Note on the Historical Character of Some Eighteenth-Century London Virginia Firms." *Wm Mar Q*, 3d ser., XIX (1962), 400-407.

10 ROBERTSON, M. L. "Scottish Commerce and the American War of Independence." *Econ Hist Rev*, 2d ser., IX (1956), 123-131.

11 ROSENBLATT, Samuel M. "The Significance of Credit in the Tobacco Consignment Trade: A Study of John Norton and Sons, 1768-1775." *Wm Mar Q*, 3d ser., XIX (1962), 383-399.

12 SCHUMPETER, Elizabeth B. *English Overseas Trade Statistics, 1697-1808*. Oxford, 1960.

13 SHERIDAN, R. B. "The Commercial and Financial Organization of the British Slave Trade, 1750-1807." *Econ Hist Rev*, 2d ser., XI (1958), 249-263.

14 THOMAS, Robert P. "The Sugar Colonies of the Old Empire: Profit or Loss for Great Britain?" *Econ Hist Rev*, 2d ser., XXI (1968), 30-45.

15 WARD, William R. *The English Land Tax in the Eighteenth Century*. Oxford, 1953.

C. SOCIAL AND CULTURAL ASPECTS

16 ADAMS, Margaret I. "The Highland Emigration of 1770." *Scottish Hist Rev*, XVI (1918-1919), 280-293.

17 BRIDENBAUGH, Carl. *Mitre and Sceptre: Transatlantic Faiths, Ideas, Personalities, and Politics, 1689-1775*. New York, 1962.†

18 CAMPBELL, Mildred. "English Emigration on the Eve of the American Revolution." *Am Hist Rev*, LXI (1955), 1-20.

1 CLIVE, John, and Bernard BAILYN. "England's Cultural Provinces: Scotland and America." *Wm Mar Q*, 3d ser., XI (1954), 200-213.

2 CONNELY, Willard. "Colonial Americans in Oxford and Cambridge." *Am Ox*, XXIX (1942), 6-17, 75-77.

3 CROSS, Arthur L. *The Anglican Episcopate and the American Colonies.* New York, 1902.

4 GEORGE, M. D. "America in English Satirical Prints." *Wm Mar Q*, 3d ser., X (1953), 511-537.

5 GREEN, E. R. R. "Scotch-Irish Emigration, an Imperial Problem." *W Pa Hist Mag*, XXXV (1952), 193-209.

6 HARLAN, Robert. "William Strahan's American Book Trade, 1744-1776." *Lib Q*, XXXI (1961), 235-244.

7 KRAUS, Michael. *The Atlantic Civilization: Eighteenth-Century Origins.* Ithaca, N.Y., 1949.†

8 MELLOR, George R. "Emigration from the British Isles to the New World, 1765-1775." *History*, XL (1955), 68-83.

9 RAZZELL, P. E. "Population Change in Eighteenth-Century England: A Reinterpretation." *Econ Hist Rev*, 2d ser., XVIII (1965), 312-332.

10 ROBBINS, Caroline. *The Eighteenth-Century Commonwealth Man.* Cambridge, Mass., 1959.†

11 SACHSE, William L. *The Colonial American in Britain.* Madison, 1956.

12 SOSIN, Jack M. "The Proposal in the Pre-Revolutionary Decade for Establishing Anglican Bishops in the Colonies." *J Econ Hist*, XIII (1962), 76-84.

13 TOLLES, Frederick B. *Quakers and the Atlantic Culture.* New York, 1960.

D. COLONIAL POLICY TO 1763

14 ANDREWS, Charles M. *England's Commercial and Colonial Policy.* Vol. IV of *The Colonial Period of American History.* New Haven, 1938.†

15 BOND, Beverley, W., Jr. *The Quit-Rent System in the American Colonies.* New Haven, 1919.

16 DICKERSON, Oliver M. *The Navigation Acts and the American Revolution.* Philadelphia, 1951.†

17 GRAHAM, Gerald S. *Empire of the North Atlantic: The Maritime Struggle for North America.* 2d ed. Toronto, 1958.

18 GRAMPP, William D. "The Liberal Elements in English Mercantilism." *Q J Econ*, LXVI (1952), 465-501.

1 HARPER, Lawrence A. "The Effect of the Navigation Acts on the Thriteen Colonies." In *The Era of the American Revolution*, ed. Richard B. Morris. New York, 1939.

2 HARPER, Lawrence A. "Mercantilism and the American Revolution." *Canad Hist Rev*, XXIII (1942), 1-16.

3 KAMMEN, Michael. *Empire and Interest: The American Colonies and the Politics of Mercantilism*. New York, 1970.†

4 MALONE, Joseph J. *Pine Trees and Politics: The Naval Stores and Forest Policy in Colonial New England, 1691-1775*. Seattle, 1964.

5 RANSOM, Roger L. "British Policy and Colonial Growth: Some Implications of the Burden from the Navigation Acts." *J Econ Hist*, XXVIII (1968), 427-435.

6 SOUTHWICK, Albert B. "The Molasses Act: Source of Precedents." *Wm Mar Q*, 3d ser., VIII (1951), 389-405.

7 THOMAS, Robert P. "British Imperial Policy and the Economic Interpretation of the American Revolution." *J Econ Hist*, XXVIII (1968), 436-440.

8 THOMAS, Robert P. "A Quantitative Approach to the Study of the Effects of British Imperial Policy upon Colonial Welfare: Some Preliminary Findings." *J Econ Hist*, XVIII (1965), 615-638.

9 VINER, Jacob. "Power Versus Plenty as Objectives of Foreign Policy in the Seventeenth and Eighteenth Centuries." *Wor Pol* I (1948), 1-29.

10 WILLIAMS, Justin. "English Mercantilism and Carolina Naval Stores, 1705-1776." *J S Hist*, I (1935), 169-185.

11 WILSON, Charles H. "'Mercantilism': Some Vicissitudes of an Idea." *Econ Hist Rev*, 2d ser., X (1957-1958), 181-188.

E. THE POLITICS OF EMPIRE

12 BLACK, Eugene C. *The Association: British Extraparliamentary Political Organization, 1769-1793*. Cambridge, Mass., 1963.

13 BOULTON, James T. *The Language of Politics in the Age of Wilkes and Burke*. London and Toronto, 1963.

14 CHRISTIE, Ian R. *Wilkes, Wyvill, and Reform: The Parliamentary Movement in British Politics, 1760-1785*. London and New York, 1962.

15 CLARK, Dora M. *British Opinion and the American Revolution*. New Haven, 1930.

16 FOORD, Archibald S. *His Majesty's Opposition, 1714-1830*. Oxford, 1964.

17 GUTTRIDGE, G. H. *English Whiggism and the American Revolution*. Berkeley and Los Angeles, 1942.†

1 NAMIER, Sir Lewis. *Crossroads of Power: Essays on Eighteenth-Century England.* London, 1962.

2 NAMIER, Sir Lewis. *England in the Age of the American Revolution.* 2d ed. London, 1961.†

3 NAMIER, Sir Lewis. *The Structure of Politics at the Accession of George III.* 2d ed. London, 1957.†

4 PLUMB, J. H. *The Growth of Political Stability in England, 1675-1725.* London, 1967.†

5 REA, Robert R. *The English Press in Politics, 1760-1774.* 1963.

6 ROSE, Robert B. "Eighteenth Century Price Riots and Public Policy in England." *Int Rev Soc Hist*, VI (1961), 277-292.

7 SUTHERLAND, Lucy S. *The City of London and the Opposition to Government, 1768-1774: A Study in the Rise of Metropolitan Radicalism.* London, 1959.

8 SUTHERLAND, Luch S. "The City of London in Eighteenth-Century Politics." In *Essays Presented to Sir Lewis Namier*, ed. Richard Pares and A. J. P. Taylor. London, 1956.

9 SUTHERLAND, Luch S. *The East India Company in Eighteenth-Century Politics.* Oxford, 1952.

10 WATSON, J. Steven. "Parliamentary Procedure as a Key to the Understanding of Eighteenth-Century Politics." *Burke Newsletter*, III (1962), 107-129.

11 WILKES, John W. "British Politics Preceding the American Revolution." *Hunt Lib Q*, XX (1956-1957), 301-319.

2. The Effects of the Great War, 1754 - 1763

A. IN BRITAIN

12 BARROW, Thomas C. "Background to the Grenville Program." *Wm Mar Q*, 3d ser., XXII (1965), 93-104.

13 BEER, George L. *British Colonial Policy, 1754-1765.* New York, 1907.

14 GIPSON, Lawrence H. "The American Revolution as an Aftermath of the Great War for the Empire, 1754-1763." *Pol Sci Q*, LXV (1950), 86-104.

15 GRANT, Charles S. "Pontiac's Rebellion and the British Troop Moves of 1763." *Miss Val Hist Rev*, LX (1953), 75-88.

16 GRANT, William L. "Canada Versus Guadeloupe, an Episode of the Seven Years' War." *Am Hist Rev*, XVII (1912), 735-743.

17 HIGONNET, Patrice Louis-René. "The Origins of the Seven Years' War." *J Mod Hist*, XL (1968), 57-90.

18 JOHN, A. H. "War and the English Economy, 1700-1763." *Econ Hist Rev*, 2d ser., VII (1954-1955), 329-344.

1   MC DERMOTT, Eric. "The Elder Pitt and His Admirals and Generals." *Mil Affairs*. XX (1956), 65-71.

2   MIDDLETON, C. R. "A Reinforcement for North America, Summer 1757." *Bull Inst Hist Res*, XLI (1968), 58-72.

3   OLSON, Alison G. "The British Government and Colonial Union, 1754." *Wm Mar Q*, 3d ser., XVII (1960), 22-34.

4   PARES, Richard. "American Versus Continental Warfare, 1739-1763." *Eng Hist Rev*, LI (1936), 429-465.

5   PARES, Richard. *Colonial Blockade and Neutral Rights, 1739-1763*. Oxford, 1938.

6   PARES, Richard. *War and Trade in the West Indies, 1739-1763*. Oxford, 1936.

7   PEASE, Theodore C. "The Mississippi Boundary of 1763: A Reappraisal of Responsibility." *Am Hist Rev*, XL (1935), 278-286.

8   RASHED, Zenab E. *The Peace of Paris, 1763*. Liverpool, Eng., 1951.

9   RUSSELL, Nelson V. "The Reaction in England and America to the Capture of Havana, 1762." *His-Am Hist Rev*, IX (1929), 303-316.

10   SAVELLE, Max. *The Origins of American Diplomacy: The International History of Anglo-America, 1492-1763*. New York, 1967.

11   WADDINGTON, Richard. *La Guerre de Sept Ans: Histoire Diplomatique et Militaire*. 5 vols. Paris, 1899-1914.

B. IN AMERICA

12   BAKERS-CROTHERS, Hayes. *Virginia and the French and Indian War*. Chicago, 1928.

13   BERG, Harry D. "Economic Consequences of the French and Indian War for the Philadelphia Merchants." *Pa Hist*, XIII (1946), 185-193.

14   FREGAULT, Guy. *La Guerre de la Conquête*. Montreal, 1955.

15   GIPSON, Lawrence H. "Connecticut Taxation and Parliamentary Aid Preceding the Revolutionary War." *Am Hist Rev*, XXXVI (1930-1931), 721-739.

16   GIPSON, Lawrence H. "A View of the Thirteen Colonies at the Close of the Great War for the Empire, 1763." *N Y Hist*, XL (1959), 327-357.

17   GREENE, Jack P. "The South Carolina Quartering Dispute, 1757-1758." *S C Hist Mag*, LX (1959), 193-204.

18   JOHNSON, Victor L. "Fair Traders and Smugglers in Philadelphia, 1754-1763." *Pa Mag Hist*, LXXXIII (1959), 125-149.

19   KETCHAM, Ralph L. "Conscience, War, and Politics in Pennsylvania, 1755-1757." *Wm Mar Q*, 3d ser., XX (1963), 416-439.

1 LONG, John C. *Lord Jeffery Amherst, a Soldier of the King.* New York, 1933.

2 MC CARDELL, Lee. *Ill-Starred General: Braddock of the Coldstream Guards.* Pittsburgh, 1958.†

3 PARGELLIS, Stanley M. "Braddock's Defeat." *Am Hist Rev*, XLI (1936), 253-269.

4 PARGELLIS, Stanley M. *Lord Loudoun in North America.* New Haven and London, 1933.

5 PARKMAN, Francis. *Montcalm and Wolfe.* 2 vols. Boston, 1884.

6 SCHUTZ, John A. *William Shirley: King's Governor of Massachusetts.* Chapel Hill, 1961.

7 SIEBERT, Wilbur H. "Spanish and French Privateering in Southern Waters, July, 1762, to March, 1763." *Ga Hist Q*, XVI (1932), 163-178.

8 THAYER, Theodore G. "The Army Contractors for the Niagara Campaign, 1755-1756." *Wm Mar Q*, 3d ser., XIV (1957), 31-46.

9 WEAVER, Glenn. "The German Reformed Church During the French and Indian War." *J Presby Hist Soc*, XXXV (1957), 265-277.

10 YOUNG, Chester R. "The Stress of War upon the Civilian Population of Virginia, 1739-1760." *W Va Hist*, XXVII (1966), 251-277.

3. The Impulse for Change

A. IDEAS

11 BAILYN, Bernard. *Origins of American Politics.* New York, 1967.

12 BARKER, Sir Ernest. "Natural Law and the American Revolution." In *Traditions of Civility.* Cambridge, 1948.

13 CHRISTIE, Ian R. "Was There a 'New Toryism' in the Earlier Part of George III's Reign?" *J Brit Stud*, V (1965), 60-76.

14 DUFF, Stella F. "The Case Against the King: *The Virginia Gazettes* Indict George III." *Wm Mar Q*, 3d ser., VI (1949), 383-397.

15 ERICSON, Frederic J. *The British Colonial System and the Question of Change of Policy on the Eve of the Revolution.* Chicago, 1943.

16 FIELDHOUSE, David. "British Imperialism in the Late Eighteenth Century: Defence or Opulence." In *Essays in Imperial Government*, ed. K. Robinson and F. Madden. Oxford, 1963.

1   GREENE, Jack P. "Political Mimesis: A Consideration of the Historical and Cultural Roots of Legislative Behaviour in the British Colonies in the Eighteenth Century." *Am Hist Rev*, LXXV (1969), 337-360. With Bernard Bailyn, "A Comment," 361-363, and Greene, "Reply," 364-367.

2   KATZ, Stanley N. "The Origins of American Constitutional Thought." *Perspectives in American History*, III (1969), 474-490.

3   KEITH, A. B. *Constitutional History of the First British Empire*. Oxford, 1930.

4   KNORR, Klaus E. *British Colonial Theories, 1570-1850*. Toronto, 1944.

5   KOEBNER, Richard. *Empire*. Cambridge, 1961.†

6   MC ILWAIN, Charles H. *The American Revolution: A Constitutional Interpretation*. New York, 1923.†

7   MATTEUCCI, Nicola. *Charles Howard McIlwain e la storiografia sulla rivoluzione Americana*. Bologna, 1965.

8   MARTIN, Chester B. *Empire and Commonwealth: Studies in Governance and Self-Government in Canada*. Oxford, 1929.

9   MULLET, Charles F. "English Imperial Thinking, 1764-1783." *Pol Sci Q*, XLV (1930), 548-579.

10   POCOCK, J. G. A. "Machiavelli, Harrington and English Political Ideologies in the Eighteenth Century." *Wm Mar Q*, 3d ser., XXII (1965), 547-583.

11   ROBBINS, Caroline. *The Eighteenth-Century Commonwealthman*. Cambridge, Mass., 1959.†

12   ROBERTSON, Sir Charles G. "The Imperial Problem in North America in the Eighteenth Century (1914-1783)." *U Birmingham Hist J*, I (1947), 134-157.

13   SCHUYLER, Robert L. "British Imperial Theory and American Territorial Policy: A Suggested Relationship." *Proc Am Philos Soc*, XCVII (1953), 317-331.

14   SCHUYLER, Robert L. *Parliament and the British Empire: Some Constitutional Controversies Concerning Imperial Legislative Jurisdiction*. New York, 1929.

15   SHY, John "Thomas Pownall, Henry Ellis, and the Spectrum of Possibilities, 1763-1775." In *Anglo-American Political Relations*, ed. Alison G. Olson. New Brunswick, 1970.

16   WHEELER, Harvey. "Calvin's Case (1608) and the McIlwain-Schyyler Debate." *Am Hist Rev*, LXI (1956), 587-597.

B. PRESSURE GROUPS

√ 17   APPLETON, Marguerite. "The Agents of the New England Colonies in the Revolutionary Period." , *VI (1933), 371-387.*

1 BARNWELL, Joseph W. "Hon. Charles Garth, M.P., the Last Colonial Agent of South Carolina in England, and Some of His Work." *S C Hist Mag*, XXVI (1925), 67-92.

2 BUMSTED, John M. "Doctor Douglass' Summary: Polemic for Reform, 2." *N Eng Q*, XXXVII (1964), 242-250.

3 FREIBURG, Malcolm. "William Bollan: Agent of Massachusetts." *More Books*, XXIII (1949), 43-53, 90-100, 135-146, 168-182, 212-220.

4 JERVEY, Theodore D. "Barlow Trecothick." *S C Hist Mag*, XXXII (1931), 157-169.

5 KAMMEN, Michael G. *A Rope of Sand: The Colonial Agents, British Politics, and the American Revolution*. Ithaca, N.Y., 1968.

6 NAMIER, Sir Lewis. "Charles Garth and His Connections." *Eng Hist Rev*, LIV (1939), 443-470, 632-652.

7 PENSON, Lilian M. "The London West India Interest in the Eighteenth Century." *Eng Hist Rev*, XXXVI (1921), 373-392.

8 RICH, R. E. *The History of the Hudson's Bay Company, 1670-1870*. 2 vols. London, 1958-1959.

9 SCOTT, S. Morley. "Civil and Military Authority in Canada, 1764-1766." *Canad Hist Rev*, IX (1928), 117-136.

10 SOSIN, Jack M. *Agents and Merchants: British Colonial Policy and the Origins of the American Revolution, 1763-1775*. Lincoln, Neb., 1965.

11 TAYLOR, Robert J. "Israel Mauduit." *N Eng Q*, XXIV (1951), 208-230.

12 CARGA, Nicholas. "Robert Charles, New York Agent, 1748-1770." *Wm Mar Q*, 3d ser., XVIII (1961), 211-235.

C. BRITISH POLITICS AND COLONIAL POLICY, 1763-1765

13 ALVORD, Clarence W. *The Mississippi Valley in British Politics: A Study of the Trade, Land Speculation, and Experiments in Imperialism Culminating in the American Revolution*. 2 vols. Cleveland, 1917.

14 BARROW, Thomas C. "A Project for Imperial Reform: 'Hints Respecting the Settlement for Our American Provinces,' 1763." *Wm Mar Q*, 3d ser., XXIV (1967), 108-126.

15 CARTER, Clarence E. "The Significance of the Military Office in America, 1763-1775." *Am Hist Rev*, XXVIII (1923), 475-488.

16 CHRISTIE, Ian R. "The Cabinet During the Grenville Administration, 1763-1765." *Eng Hist Rev*, LXXIII (1958), 86-91.

17 ERICSON, Frederic J. "The Contemporary British Opposition to the Stamp Act, 1764-65." *Pap Mich Ac Sc Ar Let*, XXIX (1943), 489-505.

1 ERNST, Joseph A. "Genesis of the Currency Act of 1764: Virginia Paper Money and the Protection of British Investments." *Wm Mar Q*, 3d ser., XXII (1965), 33-74.

2 *HUGHES, Edward. "The English Stamp Duties, 1664-1764." Eng Hist Rev*, LVI (1941), 234-264.

3 HUMPHREYS, R. A. "Lord Shelburne and the Proclamation of 1763." *Eng Hist Rev*, XLIX (1934), 241-264.

4 JOHNSON, Allen S. "The Passage of the Sugar Act." *Wm Mar Q*, 3d ser., XVI (1959), 507-514.

5 JOHNSON, Victor L. "Internal Financial Reform or External Taxation: Britain's Fiscal Choice, 1763." *Proc Am Philos Soc*, XCVIII (1954), 31-7.

6 MORGAN, Edmund S. "The Postponement of the Stamp Act." *Wm Mar Q*, 3d ser., VII (1950), 353-392.

7 RITCHESON, Charles R. "The Preparation of the Stamp Act." *Wm Mar Q*, 3d ser., X (1953), 543-559.

8 SOSIN, Jack M. "A Postscript to the Stamp Act, George Grenville's Revenue Measures: A Drain on Colonial Specie?" *Am Hist Rev*, LXIII (1958), 918-923.

9 SOSIN, Jack M. *Whitehall and the Wilderness: The Middle West in British Colonial Policy, 1760-1775.* Lincoln, Neb., 1961.

10 WOLKINS, George G. "Writs of Assistance in England." *Proc Mass Hist Soc*, LXVI (1936-1941), 357-364.

V. The Coming of the Revolution, 1765 - 1775

1. General Works

11 ADAMS, Randolph G. *Political Ideas of the American Revolution: Britannic-American Contributions to the Problem of Imperial Organization, 1765-1775.* Durham, N.C., 1922.

12 SCHUYLER, Robert L. "The Britannic Question and the American Revolution." *Pol Sci Q*, XXXVIII (1923), 104-114. (Review of R. G. Adams.)

13 BAILYN, Bernard, ed. *Pamphlets of the American Revolution, 1750-1776, Volume I: 1750-1765.* Cambridge, Mass., 1965. See 95.3.

14 BASCHWITZ, Kurt. "Schreckensherrschaften und ihre Presse; Eine Zeitungs-Geschichtliche Studie." *Int Rev Soc Hist*, I (1936), 273-310.

15 DICKERSON, Oliver M. "British Control of American Newspapers on the Eve of the Revolution." *N Eng Q*, XXIV (1951), 453-468.

16 GIPSON, Lawrence H. *The British Empire Before the American Revolution*, Vols. IX-XII. New York, 1956-1965.

1 GIPSON, Lawrence H. *The Coming of the Revolution, 1763-1775.* New York, 1954.†

2 GOEBEL, Dorothy Burne. "The 'New England Trade' and the French West Indies, 1763-1774: A Study in Trade Policies." *Wm Mar Q,* 3d ser., XX (1963), 331-372.

3 GREENE, Jack P., and Richard M. JELLISON. "The Currency Act of 1764 in Imperial-Colonial Relations, 1764-1776." *Wm Mar Q,* 3d ser., XVIII (1961), 485-518.

4 GREENOUGH, Chester N. "New England Almanacs, 1766-1775, and the American Revolution." *Proc Am Ant Soc,* n.s., XLV (1936), 288-316.

5 HINKHOUSE, Fred J. *The Preliminaries of the American Revolution as Seen in the English Press, 1763-1775.* New York, 1926.

6 HOWARD, George E. *Preliminaries of the Revolution, 1763-1775.* New York, 1905.

7 JENSEN, Merrill. *The Founding of a Nation: A History of the American Revolution, 1763-1776.* New York, 1968.

8 LOVEJOY, David S. "Rights Imply Equality: The Case Against Admiralty Jurisdiction in America, 1764-1776." *Wm Mar Q,* 3d ser., XVI (1959), 459-484.

9 MARTIN, Alfred S. "The King's Customs: Philadelphia, 1763-1774." *Wm Mar Q,* 3d ser., V (1948), 201-216.

10 MILLER, John C. *Origins of the American Revolution.* Stanford, 1959.†

11 SCHLESINGER, Arthur M. *The Colonial Merchants and the American Revolution, 1763-1776.* New York, 1918.

12 SCHLESINGER, Arthur M. "A Note on Songs as Patriot Propaganda, 1765-1776." *Wm Mar Q,* 3d ser., XI (1954), 78-88.

13 SCHLESINGER, Arthur M. "Political Mobs and the American Revolution, 1765-1776." *Proc Am Philos Soc,* XCIX (1955), 244-250.

14 SCHLESINGER, Arthur M. *Prelude to Independence: The Newspaper War on Britain, 1764-1776.* New York, 1958.

15 SHY, John. *Toward Lexington: The Role of the British Army in the Coming of the American Revolution.* Princeton, 1965.†

16 SOSIN, Jack M. "Imperial Regulation of Colonial Paper Money, 1764-1773." *Pa Mag Hist,* LXXXVIII (1964), 174-198.

17 STOUT, Neil R. "Manning the Royal Navy in North America, 1763-1775." *Am Neptune,* XXIII (1963), 174-185.

18 TATE, Thad W. "The Coming of the Revolution in Virginia: Britain's Challenge to Virginia's Ruling Class, 1763-1776." *Wm Mar Q,* 3d ser., XIX (1963), 323-343.

19 UBBELOHDE, Carl. *The Vice-Admiralty Courts and the American Revolution.* Chapel Hill, 1960.

1 YOUNGER, Richard D. "Grand Juries and the American Revolution." *Va Mag Hist*, LXII (1955), 257-268.

2. American Resistance Before the Stamp Act

2 CONNOLLY, James G. "Quit-Rents in Colonial New Jersey as a Contributing Cause for the American Revolution." *Proc N J Hist Soc*, n.s. VII (1922), 13-21.

3 ERNST, Joseph A. "The Currency Act Repeal Movement: A Study of Imperial Politics and Revolutionary Crisis, 1764-1767." *Wm Mar Q*, 3d ser., XXV (1968), 177-211.

4 FIORE, Jordan D. "The Temple-Bernard Affair: A Royal Custom House Scandal in Essex County." *Essex Inst Hist Coll*, XC (1954), 58-83.

5 GIPSON, Lawrence H. "Aspects of the Beginning of the American Revolution in Massachusetts Bay, 1760-1762." *Proc Am Ant Soc*, LXVII (1957), 11-32.

6 HICKMAN, Emily. "Colonial Writs of Assistance." *N Eng Q*, V (1932), 83-104.

7 JACOBSON, David L. "John Dickinson's Fight Against Royal Government, 1764." *Wm Mar Q*, 3d ser., XIX (1962), 64-85.

8 JOHNSON, Herbert A., and David SYRETT. "Some Nice Sharp Quillets of the Customs Law: The *New York* Affair, 1763-1767." *Wm Mar Q*, 3d ser., XXV (1968), 432-451.

9 KING, Joseph E. "Judicial Flotsam in Massachusetts-Bay, 1760-1765." *N Eng Q*, XXVII (1954), 366-381.

10 KLEIN, Milton M. "Prelude to Revolution in New York: Jury Trials and Judicial Tenure." *Wm Mar Q*, 3d ser., XVII (1960), 439-462.

11 KNOLLENBERG, Bernhard. *Origin of the American Revolution, 1759-1766*. New York, 1960.†

12 MORGAN, Edmund S. "Colonial Ideas of Parliamentary Power, 1764-1766." *Wm Mar Q*, 3d ser., V (1948), 311-341.

13 NADELHAFT, Jerome J. "Politics and the Judicial Tenure Fight in Colonial New Jersey." *Wm Mar Q*, 3d ser., XXVIII (1971), 46-63.

14 WATERS, John J., and John A. SCHUTZ. "Patterns of Massachusetts Colonial Politics: The Writs of Assistance and the Rivalry Between the Otis and Hutchinson Families." *Wm Mar Q*, 3d ser., XXIV (1967), 543-567.

15 WEIR, Robert M. "North Carolina's Reaction to the Currency Act of 1764." *N C Hist Rev*, XL (1963), 183-199.

16 WIENER, Frederick B. "The Rhode Island Merchants and the Sugar Act." *N Eng Q*, III (1930), 465-500.

17 WOLKINS, George G. "Daniel Malcolm and Writs of Assistance." *Proc Mass Hist Soc*, LVIII (1924-1925), 5-84.

3. The Stamp Act Crisis, 1765 - 1766

1 ADAIR, Douglass. "The Stamp Act in Contemporary English Cartoons." *Wm Mar Q*, 3d ser., X (1953), 538-542.

2 ANDERSON, George P. "Ebenezer Mackintosh: Stamp Act Rioter and Patriot." *Pub Col Soc Mass*, XXVI (1924-1926), 15-64.

3 ANDERSON, George P. "A Note on Ebenezer Mackintosh." *Pub Col Soc Mass*, XXVI (1924-1926), 348-361.

4 CHROUST, Anton-Hermann. "The Lawyers of New Jersey and the Stamp Act." *Am J Leg Hist*, VI (1962), 286-297.

5 CRANE, Verner W. "Benjamin Franklin and the Stamp Act." *Pub Col Soc Mass*, XXXII (1933-1937), 56-77.

6 DAVIDSON, Philip G. "Sons of Liberty and Stamp Men." *N C Hist Rev*, IX (1932), 38-56.

7 D'INNOCENZO, Michael, and John J. TURNER, Jr. "The Role of New York Newspapers in the Stamp Act Crisis, 1764-66." *N-Y Hist Soc Q*, LI (1967), 215-231, 345-365.

8 ELLEFSON, C. Ashley. "The Stamp Act in Georgia." *Ga Hist Q*, XLVI (1962), 1-19.

9 ENGLEMAN, F. L. "Cadwallader Colden and the New York Stamp Act Riots." *Wm Mar Q*, 3d ser., X (1953), 560-578.

10 GIDDENS, Paul H. "Maryland and the Stamp Act Controversy." *Md Hist Mag*, XXVII (1932), 79-98.

11 GIPSON, Lawrence H. "The Great Debate in the Committee of the Whole House of Commons on the Stamp Act, 1766, as Reported by Nathaniel Ryder." *Pa Mag Hist*, LXXXVI (1962), 10-41.

12 GRANGER, Bruce I. "The Stamp Act in Satire." *Am Q*, VIII (1956), 368-384.

13 HAYWOOD, C. Robert. "The Mind of North Carolina Opponents of the Stamp Act." *N C Hist Rev*, XXIX (1952), 317-343.

14 JOHNSON, Ellen S. "British Politics and the Repeal of the Stamp Act." *S Atl Q*, LXII (1963), 169-188.

15 KERR, Wilfred B. "The Stamp Act and the Floridas, 1765-1766." *Miss Val Hist Rev*, XXI (1935), 436-470.

16 KERR, Wilfred B. "The Stamp Act in Nova Scotia." *N Eng Q*, VI (1933), 552-566.

17 KERR, Wilfred B. "The Stamp Act in Quebec." *Eng Hist Rev*, XLVII (1932), 648-651.

18 LAPRADE, William T. "The Stamp Act in British Politics." *Am Hist Rev*, XXXV (1930), 735-757.

1   LEE, E. Lawrence. "Days of Defiance: Resistance to the Stamp Act in the Lower Cape Fear." *N C Hist Rev*, XLIII (1966), 186-202.

2   LEMISCH, Jesse. "New York's Petitions and Resolves of December 1765: Liberals vs. Radicals." *N-Y Hist Soc Q*, XLIX (1965), 313-326.

3   MC ANEAR, Beverly. "The Albany Stamp Act Riots." *Wm Mar Q*, 3d ser., IV (1947), 486-498.

4   MINCHINTON, Walter E. "The Stamp Act Crisis: Bristol and Virginia." *Va Mag Hist*, LXXIII (1965), 145-155.

5   MORGAN, Edmund S. and Helen M. *The Stamp Act Crisis; Prologue to Revolution.* Chapel Hill, 1953.†

6   MORGAN, Edmund S., ed. *Prologue to Revolution: Sources and Documents on the Stamp Act Crisis, 1764-1766.* Chapel Hill, 1959.†

7   NEWCOMB, Benjamin H. "Effects of the Stamp Act on Colonial Pennsylvania Politics." *Wm Mar Q*, 3d ser., XXIII (1966), 257-272.

8   REICHENBACH, Karl H. "The Connecticut Clergy and the Stamp Act." In *University of Michigan Historical Essays*, ed. A. E. R. Boak. Ann Arbor, 1937, pp. 141-158.

9   STOUT, Neil R. "Captain Kennedy and the Stamp Act." *N Y Hist*, XLV (1964), 44-58.

10   WOODY, Robert H. "Christopher Gadsden and the Stamp Act." *Proc S C Hist Assn*, IX (1939), 7-9.

11   YOUNG, Henry J. "Agrarian Reactions to the Stamp Act in Pennsylvania." *Pa Hist*, XXIV (1967), 25-30.

4. The Townsend Acts and American Resistance, 1767 - 1770

12   ALDEN, John E. "John Mein: Scourge of Patriots." *Pub Col Soc Mass*, XXXIV (1937-1942), 571-599.

13   ANDREWS, Charles M. "The Boston Merchants and the Non-Importation Movement." *Pub Col Soc Mass*, XIX (1916-1917), 159-259.

14   ARMYTAGE, Frances. *The Free Port System in the British West Indies: A Study in Commercial Policy, 1766-1822.* London, 1953.

15   BROOKE, John. *The Chatham Administration, 1766-1768.* London and New York, 1956.

16   BRUNHOUSE, R. L. "The Effect of the Townshend Acts in Pennsylvania." *Pa Mag Hist*, LIV (1930), 355-373.

17   CHAFFIN, Robert J. "The Townshend Acts of 1767." *Wm Mar Q*, 3d ser., XXVII (1970), 90-121.

1 CHAMPAGNE, Roger. "Family Politics Versus Constitutional Principles: The New York Assembly Elections of 1768 and 1769." *Wm Mar Q*, 3d ser., XX (1963), 57-79.

2 CHANNING, Edward. "The American Board of Commissioners of the Customs." *Proc Mass Hist Soc*, XLIII (1910), 477-490.

3 CLARK, Dora Mae. "The American Board of Customs, 1767-1783." *Am Hist Rev*, XLV (1939-1940), 777-806.

4 DICKERSON, Oliver M. "The Commissioners of Customs and the 'Boston Massacre.'" *N Eng Q*, XXVII (1954), 307-325.

5 DICKERSON, Oliver M. "Use Made of the Revenue from the Tax on Tea." *N Eng Q*, XXXL (1958), 232-243.

6 DICKERSON, Oliver M., ed. *Boston Under Military Rule, 1768-1769: As Revealed in a "Journal of the Times."* Boston, 1936.

7 FRESE, Joseph R. "Some Observations on the American Board of Customs Commissioners." *Proc Mass Hist Soc*, LXXXI (1969), 3-30.

8 HENDERSON, Patrick. "Smallpox and Patriotism: The Norfolk Riots, 1768-1769." *Va Mag Hist*, LXXIII (1965), 413-424.

9 KIDDER, Frederic. *History of the Boston Massacre, 5 March 1770.* Albany, 1870.

10 LORD, Donald C., and Robert M. CALHOON. "The Removal of the Massachusetts General Court from Boston, 1769-1772." *J Am Hist*, LV (1969), 735-755.

11 MAIER, Pauline. "John Wilkes and American Disillusionment with Britain." *Wm Mar Q*, 3d ser., XX (1963), 373-395.

12 RUDE, George. *Wilkes and Liberty: A Social Study of 1763-1774.* Oxford, 1960†

13 SMITH, Glenn C. "An Era of Non-Importation Associations, 1768-73." *Wm Mar Q*, 2d ser., XX (1940), 84-98.

14 SPECTOR, Margaret M. *The American Department of the British Government, 1768-1782.* New York, 1940.

15 THOMAS, P. D. G. "Charles Townshend and American Taxation in 1767." *Eng Hist Rev*, LXXXIII (1968), 33-51.

16 VARGA, Nicholas. "The New York Restraining Act: Its Passage and Some Effects, 1766-1768." *N Y Hist*, XXXVII (1956), 233-258.

17 WATKINS, Walter K. "Tarring and Feathering in Boston in 1770." *Old-Time N Eng*, XX (1929), 30-43.

18 WATSON, Derek. "The Rockingham Whigs and the Townshend Duties." *Eng Hist Rev*, LXXXIV (1969), 561-565.

19 WOLKINS, George G. "The Seizure of John Hancock's Sloop *Liberty*." *Proc Mass Hist Soc*, LV (1921-1922), 239-284.

20 WROTH, L. Kinvin, and Hiller B. ZOBEL, eds. *The Legal Papers of John Adams.* 3 vols. Cambridge, Mass., 1965. (See Vol. III on the Boston "Massacre" trial.)

1   ZOBEL, Hiller B. *The Boston Massacre.* New York, 1970.

2   LEMISCH, Jesse. "Radical Plot in Boston (1770): A Study in the Use of Evidence." *Harvard Law Review*, LXXXIV (1970), 485-504. (Review of Zobel.)

5. The Question of the Trans - Appalachian West

3   ABERNETHY, Thomas P. *Western Lands and the American Revolution.* New York, 1937.

4   ALDEN, John R. *John Stuart and the Southern Colonial Frontier: A Study of Indian Relations, War, Trade, and Land Problems in the Southern Wilderness, 1754-1775.* Ann Arbor, 1944.

5   ALVORD, Clarence W. *Mississippi Valley in British Politics: A Study of the Trade, Land Speculation, and Experiments in Imperialism Culminating in the American Revolution.* 2 vols. Cleveland, 1917.

6   BAILEY, Kenneth P. *The Ohio Company of Virginia and the Westward Movement, 1748-1792.* Glendale, Calif., 1939.

7   BILLINGTON, Ray A. "The Fort Stanwix Treaty of 1768." *N Y Hist*, XXV (1944), 182-194.

8   BROWN, Douglas S. "The Iberville Canal Project: Its Relation to Anglo-French Commercial Rivalry in the Mississippi Valley, 1763-1775." *Miss Val Hist Rev*, XXXII (1946), 491-516.

9   CARTER, Clarence E. *Great Britain and the Illinois Country, 1763-1774.* Washington, D.C., 1910.

10 CURRY, Richard. "Lord Dunmore and the West: A Re-evaluation." *W Va Hist*, XIX (1958), 231-243.

11 CURRY, Richard. "Lord Dunmore: Tool of Land Jobbers or Realistic Champion of Colonial 'Rights?' An Inquiry." *W Va Hist*, XXIV (1963), 289-295.

12 DEVORSEY, Louis, Jr. *The Indian Boundary in the Southern Colonies, 1763-1775.* Chapel Hill, 1966.

13 DEVORSEY, Louis, Jr. "The Virginia Cherokee Boundary of 1771." *Pub E Tenn Hist Soc*, No. 33 (1961), 17-31.

14 DOWNES, Randolph C. "Dunmore's War: An Interpretation." *Miss Val Hist Rev*, XXI (1935), 311-330.

15 FLEXNER, James T. *Mohawk Baronet: Sir William Johnson of New York.* New York, 1959.

16 HUSTON, John W. "The British Evacuation of Fort Pitt, 1772." *W Pa Hist Mag*, XLVIII (1965), 317-329.

17 JAMES, Alfred P. *George Mercer of the Ohio Company: A Study in Frustration.* Pittsburgh, 1963.

18 LEWIS, George E. *The Indiana Company, 1763-1798: A Study in Eighteenth-Century Frontier Land Speculation and Business Venture.* Glendale, Calif., 1941.

1 MARSHALL, Peter. "Lord Hillsborough, Samuel Wharton and the Ohio Grant, 1769-1775." *Eng Hist Rev*, LXXX (1965), 717-739.

2 MARHSALL, Peter. "Sir William Johnson and the Treaty of Fort Stanwix, 1768." *J Am Stud*, I (1967), 149-179.

3 PECKHAM, Howard H. *Pontiac and the Indian Uprising*. Princeton, 1947.

4 REID, Marjorie G. "The Quebec Fur-Traders and Western Policy, 1763-1774." *Canad Hist Rev*, VI (1925), 15-32.

5 RUSSELL, Nelson V. *The British Régime in Michigan and the Old Northwest, 1760-1796*. Northfield, Minn., 1939.

6 SAHLI, John R. "The Growth of British Influence Among the Seneca to 1768." *W Pa Hist Mag*, XLIX (1966), 127-139.

7 SAVELLE, Max. *George Morgan: Colony Builder*. New York, 1932.

8 SOSIN, Jack M. "The British Indian Department and Dunmore's War." *Va Mag Hist*, LXXIV (1966), 34-50.

9 SOSIN, Jack M. "The French Settlements in British Policy for the North American Interior, 1760-1774." *Canad Hist Rev*, XXXIX (1958), 185-208.

10 SOSIN, Jack M. "The Yorke-Camden Opinion and American Land Speculators." *Pa Mag Hist*, LXXXV (1961), 38-49.

11 SOSIN, Jack M. *Whitehall and the Wilderness: The Middle West in British Colonial Policy, 1760-1775*. Lincoln, Neb., 1961.

12 VAN EVERY, Dale. *Forth to the Wilderness: The First American Frontier, 1754-1774*. New York, 1961.†

13 VIRTUE, George O. *British Land Policy and the American Revolution: A Belated Lecture in Economic History*. Lincoln, Neb., 1955.

14 WAINWRIGHT, Nicholas B. *George Croghan: Wilderness Diplomat*. Chapel Hill, 1959.

15 WEBSTER, Eleanor M. "Insurrection at Fort Loudon in 1765: Rebellion or Preservation of Peace?" *W Pa Hist Mag*, XLVII (1964), 125-139.

6. The Final Crisis, 1770 - 1775

16 BARGAR, B. D. "Lord Dartmouth's Patronage, 1772-1775." *Wm Mar Q*, 3d ser., XV (1958), 191-200.

17 BARGAR, B. D. "Matthew Boulton and the Birmingham Petition of 1775." *Wm Mar Q*, 3d ser., XIII (1956), 26-39.

18 BECKER, Carl L. "The Nomination and Election of Delegates from New York to the First Continental Congress, 1774." *Pol Sci Q*, XVIII (1903), 17-46.

1 BROWN, Richard D. "Massachusetts Towns Reply to the Boston Committee of Correspondence, 1773." *Wm Mar Q*, 3d ser., XXV (1968), 22-39.

2 CHAMPAGNE, Roger. "New York and the Intolerable Acts, 1774." *N-Y Hist Sc Q*, XLV (1961), 195-207.

3 CHAPIN, Bradley. "The American Revolution as Lese Majesty." *Pa Mag Hist*, LXXIX (1955), 310-330.

4 COLLINS, E. Day. *Committees of Correspondence of the American Revolution*. Washington, D.C., 1902.

5 CORNER, Betsy C., and Dorothea W. SINGER. "Dr. John Fothergill, Peacemaker." *Proc Am Philos Soc*, XCVIII (1954), 11-22.

6 COUPLAND, Reginald. *The Quebec Act: A Study in Statesmanship*. Oxford, 1925.

7 DONOUGHUE, Bernhard. *British Politics and the American Revolution: The Path to War, 1773-75*. London and New York, 1964.

8 DRAKE, Francis S., ed. *Tea Leaves: Being a Collection of Letters and Documents Relating to the Shipment of Tea to the American Colonies in the Year 1773 by the East India Company*. Boston, 1884.

9 FAGERSTROM, Dalphy I. "Scottish Opinion and the American Revolution." *Wm Mar Q*, 3d ser., XI (1954), 252-275.

10 GERLACH, Don R. "A Note on the Quartering Act of 1774." *N Eng Q*, XXXIX (1966), 80-88.

11 GRUBER, Ira. "The American Revolution as a Conspiracy." *Wm Mar Q*, 3d ser., XXVI (1969), 360-372.

12 JAMESON, J. Franklin. "The Association." *Ann Rep Am Hist Assn for the Year 1917*. Washington, D.C., 1920, pp. 305-312.

13 KELLER, Hans G. "Pitts 'Provisional Act for Settling the Troubles in America': Das Problem der Einheit des Britischen Reiche." *Hist Zeit*, CXCIV (1962), 599-645.

14 KELLOGG, Louise Phelps. "A Footnote to the Quebec Act." *Canad Hist Rev*, XIII (1932), 147-156.

15 KNOLLENBERG, Bernhard. "Did Samuel Adams Provoke the Boston Tea Party and the Clash at Lexington?" *Proc Am Ant Soc*, n.s. LXX (1960), 493-503.

16 KNOLLENBERG, Bernhard. "John Dickinson vs. John Adams, 1774-1776." *Proc Am Philos Soc*, CVII (1963), 138-144.

17 LABAREE, Benjamin W. *The Boston Tea Party*. New York, 1964.†

18 LEAKE, James M. *The Virginia Committee System and the American Revolution*. Baltimore, 1916.

19 LESLIE, William R. "The *Gaspee* Affair: A Study of Its Constitutional Significance." *Miss Val Hist Rev*, XXXIX (1952-1953), 233-256.

1 MATTHEWS, Albert. "The Solemn League and Covenant, 1774." *Pub Col Soc Mass*, XVIII (1915-1916), 103-122.

2 METZGER, Charles H. *The Quebec Act; A Primary Cause of the American Revolution.* New York, 1936.

3 MILLER, Elmer I. "The Virginia Committee of Correspondence . . . ." *Wm Mar Q*, XXII (1913), 1-20.

4 PAGE, Elwin L. "The King's Powder, 1774." *N Eng Q*, XVIII (1945), 83-92.

5 RYAN, Frank W., Jr. "The Role of South Carolina in the First Continental Congress." *S C Hist Mag*, LX (1959), 147-153.

6 SHERIDAN, Richard B. "The British Credit Crisis of 1772 and the American Colonies." *J Econ Hist*, XX (1960), 161-186.

7 SIOUSSAT, St. George L. "The Breakdown of the Royal Management of Lands in the Southern Provinces, 1773-1775." *Ag Hist*, III (1929), 67-98.

8 SOSIN, Jack M. "The Massachusetts Act of 1774: Coercive or Preventive?" *Hunt Lib Q*, XXVI (1962-1963), 235-252.

9 STONE, Frederick D. "How the Landing of Tea Was Opposed in Philadelphia by Colonel William Bradford and Others in 1773." *Pa Mag Hist*, XV (1891), 385-393.

10 UNDERDOWN, P. T. "Henry Cruger and Edmund Burke: Colleagues and Rivals at the Bristol Election of 1774." *Wm Mar Q*, 3d ser., XV (1958), 14-34.

11 WULSIN, Eugene. "The Political Consequences of the Burning of the *Gaspee*." *R I Hist*, III (1944), 1-11. 55-64.

VI. Studies of the Revolution in Specific Communities, Colonies, States, and Regions

Bibliographical articles, where they exist, are at the head of the appropriate section.

1. New England

12 ADAMS, James T. *Revolutionary New England, 1691-1776.* Boston, 1923.

13 MAMPOTENG, Charles. "The New England Anglican Clergy in the American Revolution." *Hist Mag P E Ch*, IX (1940), 267-304.

14 WEEDEN, William B. *Economic and Social History of New England, 1620-1789.* 2 vols. Boston, 1890.

See also 1.14, 2.16, 9.2, 9.7, 11.14, 12.16, 14.1, 14.3, 19.2, 19.10, 19.11, 21.17, 23.4, 23.12, 25.11, 27.9, 31.4.

A. NEW HAMPSHIRE AND VERMONT

15 BELKNAP, Jeremy. *The History of New-Hampshire: Comprehending the Events of One Complete Century and Seventy-Five Years . . . .* 3 vols. Boston, 1813.

1 KAPLAN, Sidney. "The History of New Hampshire: Jeremy Belknap as Literary Craftsman." *Wm Mar Q*, 3d ser., XXI (1964), 18-39.

2 FAIRCHILD, Byron. *Messrs. William Pepperrell. Merchants at Piscataqua.* Ithaca, N.Y., 1954.

3 JONES, Matt B. *Vermont in the Making, 1750-1777.* Cambridge, Mass., 1939.

4 MAYO, Lawrence S. *John Wentworth, Governor of New Hampshire, 1767-1775.* Cambridge, Mass., 1921.

5 UPTON, Richard F. *Revolutionary New Hampshire: An Account of the Social and Political Forces Underlying the Transition from Royal Province to American Commonwealth.* Hanover, N.H., 1936.

6 WILLIAMSON, Chilton. *Vermont in Quandary, 1763-1825.* Montpelier, Vt., 1949.

See also 12.17, 87.12, 95.7, 98.16, 100.14.

B. MASSACHUSETTS AND MAINE

7 Boston Public Library. *The Massachusetts Bay Colony and Boston: A Selected List of Works . . . .* Boston, 1930.

8 FLAGG, Charles A. *Guide to Massachusetts Local History.* Salem, Mass., 1907.

9 BILLIAS, George A. "Beverly's Seacoast Defenses During the Revolutionary War." *Essex Inst Hist Col*, XCIV (1958), 119-131.

10 BIRDSALL, Richard D. "The Reverend Thomas Allen: Jeffersonian Calvinist." *N Eng Q*, XXX (1957), 147-165.

11 BROWN, E. Francis. *Joseph Hawley: Colonial Radical.* New York, 1931.

12 BROWN, Robert E. *Middle-Class Democracy and the Revolution in Massachusetts, 1691-1780.* Ithaca, N.Y., 1955.†

13 BULLOCK, Chandler. "More High Points in Early Worcester Politics." *Pub Worcester Hist Soc*, n.s., I (1932), 239-249.

14 CUSHING, Harry A. *History of the Transition from Provincial to Commonwealth Government in Massachusetts.* New York, 1896.

15 GOODMAN, Paul. *The Democratic Republicans of Massachusetts: Politics in a Young Republic.* Cambridge, Mass., 1964.

16 HANDLIN, Oscar and Mary. *Commonwealth: A Study of the Role of Government in the American Economy: Massachusetts, 1774-1871.* New York, 1947.

17 HART, Albert Bushnell, ed. *Commonwealth History of Massachusetts: Colony, Province and State.* 5 vols. New York, 1927-1930.

18 HUTCHINSON, Thomas. *The History of the Colony and Province of Massachusetts Bay.* Vol III. Ed. Lawrence Shaw Mayo. Cambridge, Mass., 1936.

1 LABAREE, Benjamin W. *Patriots and Partisans: The Merchants of Newburyport, 1764-1815.* Cambridge, Mass., 1962.

2 LAWSON, Murray G. "The Routes of Boston's Trade, 1752-1765." *Pub Col Soc Mass* XXXVIII (1959), 81-120.

3 NEWCOMER, Lee N. *The Embattled Farmers: A Massachusetts Countryside in the American Revolution.* New York, 1953.

4 NICHOLS, Charles L. "Samuel Salisbury—A Boston Merchant in the Revolution." *Proc Am Ant Soc* n.s. XXXV (1926), 46-63.

5 PHILLIPS, James D. "The Life and Times of Richard Derby, Merchant of Salem, 1712 to 1720." *Pub Col Soc Mass*, XXXII (1937), 514-521.

6 PHILLIPS, James D. *Salem in the Eighteenth Century.* Boston and New York, 1937.

7 POLE, J. R. "Suffrage and Representation in Massachusetts: A Statistical Note." *Wm Mar Q*, 3d ser., XIV (1957), 560-592.

8 SMITH, Marion J. *A History of Maine: From Wilderness to Statehood [1497-1820].* Portland, Me., 1949.

9 SYRETT, David. "Town-Meeting Politics in Massachusetts, 1776-1786." *Wm Mar Q*, 3d ser., XXI (1964), 352-366.

10 TAYLOR, Robert J. *Western Massachusetts in the Revolution.* Providence, 1954.

11 WALETT, Francis G. "The Massachusetts Council, 1766-1774: The Transformation of a Conservative Institution." *Wm Mar Q*, 3d ser., VI (1949), 605-627.

12 WARDEN, Gerard B. *Boston, 1689-1776.* Boston, 1970.

13 WARREN, Charles. "Elbridge Gerry, James Warren, Mercy Warren, and the Ratification of the Federal Constitution in Massachusetts." *Proc Mass Hist Soc*, LXIV (1932), 143-164.

14 WHITEHILL, Walter M. *Boston, A Topographical History.* Cambridge, Mass., 1959.

15 WINSOR, Justin, ed. *Memorial History of Boston: Including Suffolk County, Massachusetts, 1630-1880.* 4 vols. Boston, 1880-1881.

See also the biographical entries (Section VII, below) under John Adams, Samuel Adams, and John Hancock; and 9.5, 9.6, 10.8, 12.2, 12.7, 13.9, 13.15, 14.2, 14.19, 17.3, 22.2, 23.15, 23.17, 24.4, 25.3, 25.16, 26.10, 34.6, 36.3, 36.11, 39.9, 39.14, 40.2, 40.3, 41.13, 42.4, 42,6, 42.9, 42.10, 42.17, 42.19, 42.20, 43.1, 43.2, 45.1, 45.15, 45.17, 78.7, 79.10, 81.7, 81.17, 81.21, 88,14, 89.2, 96.1, 97.14, 99.7, 99.19, 101.6, 102.7, 103.7, 103.13, 103.14, 107.2.

C. CONNECTICUT

16 BUSHMAN, Richard L. *From Puritan to Yankee: Character and the Social Order in Connecticut, 1690-1765.* Cambridge, Mass., 1967.†

17 FOSTER, Stephen. "A Connecticut Separate Church: Strict Congregationalism in Cornwall, 1780-1809." *N Eng Q*, XXXIX (1966), 309-33.

18 GARVAN, Anthony N. B. *Architecture and Town Planning in Colonial Connecitcut.* New Haven, 1951.

1 GERLACH, Larry R. "Toward a 'More Perfect Union': Connecticut, the Continental Congress, and the Constitutional Convention." *Bull Conn Hist Soc*, XXXIV (1969), 65-78.

2 GRANT, Charles. *Democracy in the Connecticut Frontier Town of Kent.* New York, 1961.

3 PURCELL, Richard J. *Connecticut in Transition: 1775-1818.* Middletown, Conn., 1963.

4 TRUMBULL, Benjamin. *A Complete History of Connecticut, Civil and Ecclesiastical, from the Emigration of Its First Planters from England....* New Haven, 1818.

5 VAN DUSEN, Albert E. "Samuel Huntingdon: A Leader of Revolutionary Connecticut." *Bull Conn Hist Soc*, XIX (1954), 38-62.

6 WEAVER, Glenn. *Jonathan Trumbull, Connecticut's Merchant Magistrate, 1710-1785.* Hartford, Conn., 1956.

7 ZEICHNER, Oscar. *Connecticut's Years of Controversy, 1750-1776.* Chapel Hill, 1949.

See also 9.14, 13.1, 19.5, 20.13, 23.13, 23.16, 24.2, 26.4, 33.15, 41.8, 79.12, 79.13, 89.1, 98.6, 98.14.

D. RHODE ISLAND

8 BATES, Frank G. *Rhode Island and the Formation of the Union.* New York, 1898.

9 BRIDENBAUGH, Carl. "Colonial Newport as a Summer Resort." *R I Hist Soc Coll*, XXVI (1933), 1-23.

10 HEDGES, James B. *The Browns of Providence Plantations: Colonial Years.* Cambridge, Mass., 1952.

11 LOVEJOY, David S. *Rhode Island Politics and the American Revolution, 1760-1776.* Providence, 1958.

12 POLISHOOK, Irwin H. *1774-1795: Rhode Island and the Union.* Evanston, Ill., 1969.

13 TANNER, Earl C. "Caribbean Ports in the Foreign Commerce of Rhode Island, 1790-1830." *R I Hist*, XIV (1955), 97-108; XV (1956), 11-20.

14 WEEDEN, William B. *Early Rhode Island: A Social History of the People.* New York, 1910.

See also 13.17, 14.4, 39.16, 45.19, 46.11.

2. The Middle Atlantic Region

15 DUNBAR, Louise. "The Royal Governors in the Middle and Southern Colonies on the Eve of the Revolution: A Study in Imperial Personnel." In *The Era of the American Revolution*, ed. Richard B. Morris. New York, 1939.

1 TOLLES, Frederick B. "The Historians of the Middle Colonies." In *The Reinterpretation of Early American History*, ed. R. A. Billington. San Marino, Calif., 1966.

See also 9.9, 18.3, 20.4.

A. NEW YORK

2 ABBOTT, Wilbur C. *New York [City] in the American Revolution.* London and New York, 1929.

3 BECKER, Carl L. *The History of Political Parties in the Province of New York, 1760-1776.* Madison, 1909; repr. 1960.†

4 BECKER, E. Marie. "The 801 Westchester County Freeholders of 1763 and the Cortlandt Manor Land-Case Which Occasioned Their Listing." *N-Y Hist Soc Q*, XXXV (1951), 282-321.

5 BONOMI, Patricia U. "Political Patterns in Colonial New York City: The General Assembly Election of 1768." *Pol Sci Q*, LXXXI (1966), 432-447.

6 BROOKS, Robin. "Alexander Hamilton, Melancton Smith, and the Ratification of the Constitution in New York." *Wm Mar Q*, 3d ser., XXIV (1967), 339-358.

7 CHAMPAGNE, Roger. "Liberty Boys and Mechanics of New York City, 1764-1774." *Labor Hist*, VIII (1967), 115-135.

8 CHAMPAGNE, Roger. "The Military Association of the Sons of Liberty." *N-Y Hist Soc Q*, XLI (1957), 338-350.

9 DAWSON, Henry B. *The Sons of Liberty in New York . . . .* Poughkeepsie, 1859.

10 COCHRAN, Thomas C. *New York in the Confederation; An Economic Study.* Philadelphia, 1932.

11 DEPAUW, Linda G. *The Eleventh Pillar: New York State and the Federal Constitution.* Ithaca, N.Y., 1966.

12 FLICK, Alexander, ed. *History of the State of New York.* 10 vols. New York, 1933-1937.

13 FRIEDMAN, Bernard. "The New York Assembly Elections of 1768 and 1769: The Disruption of Family Politics." *N Y Hist*, XLVI (1965), 3-24.

14 FRIEDMAN, Bernard. "The Shaping of the Radical Consciousness in Provincial New York." *J Am Hist*, LVI (1970), 781-801.

15 GERLACH, Don K. "Philip Schuyler and the New York Frontier in 1781." *N-Y Hist Soc Q*, LIII (1969), 148-181.

16 HARRINGTON, Virginia D. "The Place of the Merchant in New York Colonial Life." *N Y Hist*, XIII (1932), 366-380.

17 JONES, Thomas. *History of New York During the Revolutionary War, and of the Leading Events in the Other Colonies at That Period.* 2 vols. New York, 1879.

1 JOHNSTON, Henry P. *Observations on Judge Jones' Loyalist History of the American Revolution.* New York, 1880.

2 KLEIN, Milton M. "Politics and Personalities in Colonial New York." *N Y Hist*, XLVII (1966), 3-16.

3 LEDER, Lawrence H. "The New York Elections of 1789: An Assault on Privilege." *Miss Val Hist Rev*, LXIX (1963), 675-682.

4 LYND, Staughton. *Anti-Federalism in Dutchess County, New York: A Study of Democracy and Class Conflict in the Revolutionary Era.* Chicago, 1962.

5 LYND, Staughton. "The Mechanics in New York Politics, 1774-1788." *Labor Hist*, V (1964), 225-246.

6 LYND, Staughton. "The Tenant Risings at Livingston Manor, May 1777." *N-Y Hist Soc Q*, XLVIII (1964), 163-177.

7 MASON, Bernard. *The Road to Independence: The Revolutionary Movement in New York, 1773-1777.* Lexington, Ky., 1966.

8 MILLS, Borden H. "Albany County's Part in the Battle of Saratoga." *Proc N Y St Hist Assn*, XV (1916), 204-224.

9 POMERANTZ, Sidney. *New York: An American City, 1783-1803.* New York, 1938.

10 SPAULDING, E. Wilder. *New York in the Critical Period, 1783-1789.* New York, 1932.

11 STOKES, I. N. Phelps. *The Iconography of Manhattan Island, 1498-1909.* 6 vols. New York, 1915-1928.

12 TEETER, Dwight L. " 'King' Sears, The Mob and Freedom of the Press in New York, 1765-76." *J Q*, XLI (1964), 539-544.

13 WERTENBAKER, Thomas J. *Father Knickerbocker Rebels: New York City During the Revolution.* New York, 1948.

14 WILSON, James G., ed. *Memorial History of the City of New York and the Hudson River Valley . . . .* 5 vols. New York, 1892-1896.

15 YOUNG, Alfred F. *The Democratic Republicans of New York: The Origins, 1763-1797.* Chapel Hill, 1967.

See also the biographical entries (Section VII, below) under Alexander Hamilton; and 10.5, 10.11, 10.15, 11.2, 12.3, 12.4, 13.2, 13.6, 13.18, 15.1, 16.14, 24.5, 25.1, 25.4, 25.12, 26.19, 36.12, 39.4, 39.5, 39.10, 40.7, 40.9, 41.2, 41.3, 42.1, 42.16, 44.18, 45.2, 78.6, 79.3, 80.14, 98.12, 102.3, 102.11, 102.17, 103.11, 105.8.

B. NEW JERSEY

16 BURR, Nelson R. *A Narrative and Descriptive Bibliography of New Jersey.* New York, Toronto, and London, 1964.

1 BURR, Nelson R. *The Anglican Church in New Jersey*. Philadelphia, 1954.

2 FISHER, Edgar J. *New Jersey as a Royal Province, 1738-1776*. New York, 1911.

3 HASKETT, Richard C. "William Patterson, Attorney General of New Jersey: Public Office and Private Profit in the American Revolution." *Wm Mar Q*, 3d ser., VII (1950), 26-38.

4 KEMMERER, Donald L. "A History of Paper Money in Colonial New Jersey, 1668-1775." *Proc N J Hist Soc*, LXXIV (1956), 107-144.

5 KEMMERER, Donald L. *Path to Freedom: The Struggle for Self-Government in Colonial New Jersey, 1703-1776*. Princeton, 1940.

6 LUNDIN, Leonard. *Cockpit of the Revolution: The War for Independence in New Jersey*. London and Princeton, 1940.

7 MC CORMICK, Richard P. *The History of Voting in New Jersey: A Study of the Development of Election Machinery, 1664-1911*. New Brunswick, 1953.

8 MC CORMICK, Richard P. *New Jersey from Colony to State, 1609-1789*. Princeton, 1964.†

9 NICHOLS, Jeanette P. "Colonial Industries of New Jersey, 1618-1815." *Am*, XXIV (1930), 299-342.

10 POLE, J. R. "Suffrage Reform and the American Revolution in New Jersey." *Proc N J Hist Soc*, LXXIV (1956), 173-194.

11 POMFRET, John E. "West New Jersey: A Quaker Society, 1675-1775." *Wm Mar Q*, 3d ser., VIII (1951), 493-519.

12 WAXHERG, Miriam E. "Money in Morris County, 1763-1782, as Indicated by Mortgage Records." *Proc N J Hist Soc*, LIII (1935), 20-26.

See also 39.2, 39.13, 40.4, 80.18, 89.12, 99.8, 101.13, 105.2.

C. PENNSYLVANIA AND DELAWARE

13 WILKINSON, Norman B., S. K. STEVENS, and D. H. KENT, eds. *Bibliography of Pennsylvania History*. 2d ed. Harrisburg, Pa., 1957.

14 BENTON, William A. "Pennsylvania Revolutionary Officers and the Federal Constitution." *Pa Hist*, XXXI (1964), 419-435.

15 BRIDENBAUGH, Carl and Jessica. *Rebels and Gentlemen: Philadelphia in the Age of Franklin*. New York, 1942.†

16 BRUNHOUSE, Robert L. *The Counter-Revolution in Pennsylvania, 1776-1790*. Harrisburg, Pa., 1942.

17 FERGUSON, Russell J. *Early Western Pennsylvania Politics [1773-1823]*. Pittsburgh, 1938.

18 FISHER, Sydney G. *Pennsylvania Colony and Commonwealth*. Philadelphia, 1897.

1 HARTZ, Louis. *Economic Policy and Democratic Thought: Pennsylvania, 1776-1860.* Cambridge, Mass., 1948.†

2 HAWKE, David. *In the Midst of a Revolution.* Philadelphia, 1961.

3 JACOBSON, David L. "The Puzzle of 'Pacificus.'" *Pa Hist*, XXXI (1964), 406-418.

4 KONKLE, Burton A. *George Bryan and the Constitution of Pennsylvania, 1731-1791.* Philadelphia, 1922.

5 LEE, Alfred M. "Dunlap and Claypole: Printers and Newsmerchants of the Revolution." *J Q*, n.s. XI (1934), 160-178.

6 LEMON, James T. "Urbanization and Development of Eighteenth-Century Southeastern Pennsylvania and Adjacent Delaware." *Wm Mar Q*, 3d ser., XXIV (1967), 501-542.

7 LINCOLN, Charles H. *The Revolutionary Movement in Pennsylvania, 1760-1776.* Philadelphia, 1901.

8 MAST, James H. "William Findley's Attempt to Move the State Capital to Harrisburg in 1787." *W Pa Hist Mag*, XXXIX (1956), 163-173.

9 MUNROE, John A. *Federalist Delaware, 1775-1815.* New Brunswick, 1954.

10 PENNINGTON, Edgar L. "The Anglican Clergy of Pennsylvania in the American Revolution.'. *Pa Mag Hist*, LXIII (1939), 401-431.

11 POLE, J. R. "Election Statistics in Pennsylvania, 1790-1840." *Pa Mag Hist*, LXXXII (1958), 217-219.

12 SCHARF, John T., and Thompson WESTCOTT. *History of Philadelphia [1609-1884].* 3 vols. Philadelphia, 1884.

13 SCHARF, John T., and others. *History of Delaware, 1609-1888.* 2 vols. Philadelphia, 1888.

14 SEED, Geoffrey. "A British Spy in Philadelphia 1775-1777." *Pa Mag*, LXXXV (1961), 3-37.

15 SELSAM, John P. *The Pennsylvania Constitution of 1776.* Philadelphia, 1936.

16 SMITH, W. Roy. "Sectionalism in Pennsylvania During the Revolution." *Pol Sci Q*, XXIV (1909), 208-235.

17 THAYER, Theodore. *Israel Pemberton, King of the Quakers.* Philadelphia, 1943.

18 THAYER, Theodore. *Pennsylvania Politics and the Growth of Democracy, 1740-1776.* Harrisburg, Pa., 1953.

19 TOLLES, Frederick B. *Meeting House and Counting House: The Quaker Merchants of Colonial Philadelphia.* Chapel Hill, 1948.†

20 WAX, Darold D. "Negro Imports into Pennsylvania, 1720-1807." *Pa Hist*, XXXII (1965), 254-287.

21 WITTLINGER, Carlton O. "The Small Arms Industry of Lancaster County, 1710-1840." *Pa Hist*, XXIV (1957), 121-136.

1 WOLF, George D. *The Fair Play Settlers of the West Branch Valley, 1769-1784: A Study of Frontier Ethnography.* Harrisburg, Pa., 1969.†

See also the biographical entries (Section VII, below), under Benjamin Franklin and John Dickinson; and 10.12, 11.10. 12.1, 12.18, 12.19, 14.13, 15.9, 15.11, 15.18, 16.17, 17.17, 17.18, 18.5, 18.6, 18.7, 18.13, 24.7, 24.10, 25.5, 25.8, 25.9, 25.17, 25.20, 33.13, 33.18, 33.19, 38.9, 39.7, 41.7, 41.11, 41.16, 46.9, 79.14, 80.8, 80.16, 80.17, 81.1, 82.5, 89.13, 101.1, 102.19.

3. The South

2 ALDEN, John R. *The First South.* Baton Rouge, 1961.

3 BERTELSON, David. *The Lazy South.* New York, 1967.

4 BRIDENBAUGH, Carl. *Myths and Realities: Societies of the Colonial South.* New York, 1963.†

5 HAYWOOD, C. Robert. "The Influence of Mercantilism on Social Attitudes in the South, 1700-1763." *J Hist Ideas*, XX (1959), 577-586.

6 MOULTRIE, William. *Memoirs of the American Revolution So Far as It Is Related to the States of North and South Carolina and Georgia: Compiled from the Most Authentic Materials.* 2 vols. New York, 1802.

7 RISJORD, Norman K. *The Old Republicans: Southern Conservatism in the Age of Jefferson.* New York, 1965.

8 ROSE, Lisle A. *Prologue to Democracy: The Federalists in the South, 1789-1800.* Lexington, Ky., 1968.

9 VER STEEG, Clarence L. "Historians and the Southern Colonies." In *The Reinterpretation of Early American History*, ed. R. A. Billington. San Marino, Calif., 1966.

See also 1.9, 2.17, 9.18, 10.6, 10.17, 18.3, 19.3, 21.9, 22.8, 24.18, 26.6, 28.2.

A. MARYLAND

10 GIDDENS, Paul H. "Bibliography on Maryland During the Time of Governor Horatio Sharpe, 1753-1769." *Md Hist Mag*, XXXI (1936), 6-16.

11 BARKER, Charles A. *The Background of the Revolution in Maryland.* New Haven, 1940.

12 BARKER, Charles A. "The Revolutionary Impulse in Maryland." *Md Hist Mag*, XXXVI (1941), 125-138.

13 BEIRNE, Rosamond Randall. "Portrait of a Colonial Governor? Robert Eden." *Md Hist Mag*, XLV (1950), 153-175, 294-311.

14 BENJAMIN, Marcus. "Maryland During the Revolution." *Md Hist Mag*, XXIV (1928), 7-15, 93-97.

1 CROWL, Philip A. *Maryland During and After the Revolution.* Baltimore, 1943.

2 GIDDENS, Paul H. "Trade and Industry in Colonial Maryland, 1753-1769." *J Econ Bus Hist*, IV (1932), 512-538.

3 HAW, James. "Maryland Politics on the Eve of Revolution: The Provincial Controversy, 1770-1773." *Md Hist Mag*, LXV (1970), 103-129.

4 POLE, J. R. "Suffrage and Representation in Maryland from 1776 to 1810: A Statistical Note and Some Reflections." *J S Hist*, XXIV (1958), 218-225.

5 SILVER, John A. "The Provisional Government of Maryland." *Stud Hist Pol Sci* (Hop), 13th ser., (1895), 481-537.

6 SKAGGS. David C. "Editorial Policies of the Maryland Gazette, 1765-1783." *Md Hist Mag*, LIX (1964), 341-349.

7 STEINER, Bernard C. "Western Maryland in the Revolution." *Stud Hist Pol Sci* (Hop), 20th ser., (1902), 2-57.

8 SULLIVAN, Kathryn. *Maryland and France, 1774-1789.* Philadelphia, 1936.

See also 11.9, 24.14, 26.2, 40.10, 78.12, 80.15, 80.19, 81.18, 102.1, 106.18.

B. VIRGINIA

9 SWEM, E. G. *Virginia Historical Index.* 2 vols. Roanoke, Va., 1934-1936.

10 CARSON, Jane. *Travelers in Tidewater Virginia, 1700-1800: A Bibliography.* Williamsburg, 1965.†

11 AMMON, Harry. "The Formation of the Republican Party in Virginia, 1789-1796." *J S Hist*, XIX (1953), 283-310.

12 AMMON, Harry. "The Jeffersonian Republicans in Virginia: An Interpretation." *Va Mag Hist*, LXXI (1963), 153-167.

13 BRIDENBAUGH, Carl. *Seat of Empire: The Political Role of Eighteenth-Century Williamsburg.* Williamsburg, 1950.†

14 BROWN, Robert E. and B. Katherine. *Virginia, 1705-1786: Democracy or Aristocracy?* East Lansing, Mich., 1964.

15 ECKENRODE, Hamilton J. *The Revolution in Virginia.* Boston and New York, 1916.

16 ERNST, Joseph A. "The Robinson Scandal Redivivus: Money, Debt, and Politics in Revolutionary Virginia." *Va Mag Hist*, LXXVII (1969), 146-173.

17 GREENE, Jack P. "The Attempt to Separate the Offices of Speaker and Treasurer in Virginia, 1758-1766." *Va Mag Hist*, LXXI (1963), 11-18.

18 GREENE, Jack P. "Foundations of Political Power in the Virginia House of Burgesses, 1720-1776." *Wm Mar Q*, 3d ser., X (1959), 485-506.

1 GRIFFITH, Lucille. *Virginia House of Burgesses, 1750-1774.* Northport, Ala., 1963.

2 HARRELL, Isaac S. "Some Neglected Phases of the Revolution in Virginia." *Wm Mar Q*, 2d ser., V (1925), 159-170.

3 HODGES, Wiley E. "Pro-Governmentalism in Virginia, 1789-1836: A Pragmatic Liberal Pattern in the Political Heritage." *J Pol*, XXV (1963), 333-360.

4 HUBBELL, Jay B., and Douglass ADAIR, eds. "Robert Mumford's *The Candidates.*" *Wm Mar Q*, 3d ser., V (1948), 217-257.

5 JEFFERSON, Thomas. *Notes on the State of Virginia*, ed. William Peden. Chapel Hill, 1955.†

6 KERCHEVAL, Samuel. *A History of the Valley of Virginia.* Westminster, Va., 1833.

7 KOONTZ, Louis K. *The Virginia Frontier, 1754-1763.* Baltimore, 1925.

8 LINGLEY, Charles R. *The Transition in Virginia from Colony to Commonwealth.* New York, 1910.

9 LOSSE, Winifred J. "The Foreign Trade of Virginia, 1789-1809." *Wm Mar Q*, 3d ser., I (1944), 161-178.

10 LOW, Augustus. *Virginia in the Critical Period, 1783-1789.* Iowa City, 1946.

11 PILCHER, George W. "Samuel Davies and the Instruction of Negroes in Virginia." *Va Mag Hist*, LXXIV (1966), 293-300.

12 POLE, J. R. "Representation and Authority in Virginia from the Revolution to Reform." *J S Hist*, XXIV (1958), 16-50.

13 REAMS, Louise A. "Taxation in Virginia During the Revolution." *Pap Richmond Col Hist*, II (1917), 43-73.

14 RISJORD, Norman K. "The Virginia Federalists." *J S Hist*, XXXIII (1967), 486-517.

15 RUTMAN, Darrett B., ed. *The Old Dominoin: Essays for Thomas Perkins Abernethy.* Charlottesville, Va., 1964.

16 SCOTT, Robert F. "Colonial Presbyterianism in the Valley of Virginia, 1727-1775." *J Presby Hist Soc*, XXXV (1957), 71-92, 171-192.

17 SOLTOW, James H. "The Role of Williamsburg in the Virginia Economy, 1750-1775." *Wm Mar Q*, 3d ser., XV (1958), 467-482.

18 SOLTOW, James H. "Scottish Traders in Virginia, 1750-1775." *Econ Hist Rev*, 2d ser., XXI (1959), 83-98.

19 SYDNOR, Charles S. *Gentlemen Freedholders: Political Practices in Washington's Virginia.* Chapel Hill, 1952.†

20 TRIMBLE, David B. "Christopher Gist and the Indian Service in Virginia, 1757-1759." *Va Mag Hist*, LXIV (1956), 143-165.

1   WERTENBAKER, Thomas J. *Norfolk: Historic Southern Port.* Durham, N.C., 1931.

2   WILLIAMS, D. Alan. "The Small Farmer in Eighteenth-Century Virginia Politics" with comment by Edward M. Riley. *Ag Hist*, LXIII (1969), 91-105.

See also the biographical entries (Section VII, below) under Patrick Henry, Thomas Jefferson, James Madison, and George Washington; and 9.8, 9.13, 10.7, 11.3, 11.6, 11.8, 12.5, 14.14, 14.16, 14.20, 17.15, 18.10, 18.11, 19.4, 19.9, 20.11, 20.12, 22.18, 23.11, 23.18, 26.5, 33.12, 34.10, 38.18, 41.4, 42.8, 45.18, 46.3, 78.14, 81.19, 87.5, 87.6, 89.9, 99.1, 104.14, 107.10, 109.6.

C. NORTH CAROLINA

3   LEFLER, Hugh T. *A Guide to the Study and Reading of North Carolina History.* Chapel Hill, 1955.†

4   ARMYTAGE, W. H. G. "The Editorial Experience of Joseph Gales, 1786-1794." *N C Hist Rev*, XXVIII (1959), 332-361.

5   BOYD, W. K. *The Federal Period, 1783-1860.* Vol. II of *History of North Carolina.* Chicago and New York, 1919.

6   CLARKE, Desmond. *Arthur Dobbs Esquire, 1689-1765: Surveyor-General of Ireland, Prospector and Governor of North Carolina.* Chapel Hill, 1957.

7   CONNOR, Robert D. W. *The Colonial and Revolutionary Periods, 1584-1783.* Vol. I of *History of North Carolina.* Chicago and New York, 1919.

8   CRITTENDEN, Charles C. *The Commerce of North Carolina, 1763-1789.* New Haven, 1936.

9   DELANEY, Norman. "The Outer Banks of North Carolina During the Revolutionary War." *N C Hist Rev*, XXXVI (1959), 1-16.

10   GANYARD, Robert L. "Radicals and Conservatives in Revolutionary North Carolina: A Point at Issue, the October Election, 1776." *Wm Mar Q*, 3d ser., XXIV (1967), 568-587.

11   HAYWOOD, C. Robert. "The Mind of the North Carolina Advocates of Mercantilism." *N C Hist Rev*, XXXIII (1955), 139-165.

12   JONES, Joseph S. *A Defense of the Revolutionary History of the State of North Carolina from the Aspersions of Mr. Jefferson.* Boston and Raleigh, 1834.

13   KAY, Marvin L. M. "The Payment of Provincial and Local Taxes in North Carolina, 1748-1771." *Wm Mar Q*, 3d ser., XXVI (1969), 328-240.

14   LONDON, Lawrence F. "The Representation Controversy in Colonial North Carolina." *N C Hist Rev*, XI (1934), 255-270.

15   MALONE, Michael T. "Sketches of the Anglican Clergy Who Served in North Carolina During the Period, 1765-1776." *Hist Mag P E Ch*, XXXIX (1970), 137-161, 399-429.

16   MERRENS, Harry R. *Colonial North Carolina in the Eighteenth Century: A Study in Historical Geography.* Chapel Hill, 1964.

1 MORRILL, James R. *The Practice and Politics of Fiat Finance: North Carolina in the Confederation, 1783-1789*. Chapel Hill, 1969.

2 NEWSOME, Albert R. "North Carolina's Ratification of the Federal Constitution." *N C Hist Rev*, XVII (1940), 287-301.

3 POOL, William C. "An Economic Interpretation of the Ratification of the Federal Constitution in North Carolina." *N C Hist Rev*, XXVII (1950), 119-141, 289-313, 437-461.

4 SELLERS, Charles G., Jr. "Making a Revolution: The North Carolina Whigs, 1765-1775." In *Studies in Southern History in Memory of Albert Ray Newsome . . .* , ed. J. Carlyle Sitterson. *James Sprunt Studies in History and Political Science*, XXXIX (1957), 23-46.

5 SKAGGS, Marvin L. *North Carolina Boundary Disputes Involving Her Southern Line*. Chapel Hill, 1941.
See also 19.6, 20.9, 23.14, 24.17, 25.7, 25.15, 26.3, 39.15, 40.13, 41.4, 82.3, 82.4, 89.4, 91.9, 98.5, 102.12, 103.1.

D. SOUTH CAROLINA

6 EASTERBY, J. H. *Guide to the Study and Reading of South Carolina History: A General Classified Bibliography*. Columbia, S.C., 1950.

7 DRAYTON, John. *Memoirs of the American Revolution*. 2 vols. Charleston, 1821.

8 GREENE, Jack P. "Bridge to Revolution: The Wilkes Fund Controversy in South Carolina, 1769-1775." *J S Hist*, XXIX (1963), 19-52.

9 GREENE, Jack P. "The Gadsen Election Controversy and the Revolutionary Movement in South Carolina." *Miss Val Hist Rev*, XLVI (1959), 469-492.

10 MC CRADY, Edward. *The History of South Carolina Under the Royal Government, 1719-1776*. London and New York, 1899.

11 PHILLIPS, Ulrich B. "The South Carolina Federalist." *Am Hist Rev*, XIV (1909), 529-543.

12 RAMSAY, David. *The History of South Carolina from Its First Settlement in 1670 to the Year 1808*. 2 vols. Charleston, 1809.

13 ROGERS, George C., Jr. "Aedanus Burke, Nathanael Greene, Anthony Wayne, and the British Merchants of Charleston." *S C Hist Mag*, LXVII (1966), 75-83.

14 SCHAPER, William A. "Sectionalism and Representation in South Carolina." *Ann Rep Am Hist Assn*, I (1900), 237-463.

15 SIRMANS, M. Eugene. *Colonial South Carolina: A Political History, 1663-1763*. Chapel Hill, 1966.

16 SMITH, William R. *South Carolina as a Royal Province, 1719-1776*. London and New York, 1903.

1 TAYLOR, George R. "Wholesale Commodity Prices at Charleston, South Carolina, 1732-1791; 1796-1861." *J Econ Bus Hist*, IV (1932), 356-377.

2 VOIGT, Gilbert P. "Religious Conditions Among German-Speaking Settlers in South Carolina, 1732-1774." *S C Hist Mag*, LVI (1955), 59-66.

3 WALLACE, David D. *The History of South Carolina*. 4 vols. New York, 1934.

4 WALSH, Richard. *Charleston's Sons of Liberty: A Study of the Artisans, 1763-1789*. Columbia, S.C., 1959.†

5 WEIR, Robert M. "'The Harmony We Were Famous For': An Interpretation of Pre-Revolutionary South Carolina Politics." *Wm Mar Q*, 3d ser., XXVI (1969), 473-491.

6 WEIR, Robert M. *"A Most Important Epocha." The Coming of the Revolution in South Carolina*. Charleston, 1970.†

See also 11.16, 11.20. 15.3, 15.7, 16.15, 16.16, 17.10, 18.14, 24.1, 25.6, 25.14, 33.17, 36.1, 41.10, 46.5, 79.9, 80.13, 97.9, 99.12, 100.7, 102.5, 102.16, 103.4, 104.13.

E. GEORGIA

7 ABBOT, William W. "A Cursory View of Eighteenth-Century Georgia." *S Atl Q*, LXI (1962), 339-344.

8 ABBOT, William W. *The Royal Governors of Georgia, 1754-1775*. Chapel Hill, 1959.

9 ABBOT, William W. "The Structure of Politics in Georgia, 1782-1789." *Wm Mar Q*, 3d ser., XIV (1957), 47-65.

10 COLEMAN, Kenneth. *The American Revolution in Georgia 1763-1789*. Athens, Ga., 1958.

11 DANIEL, Marjorie L. *The Revolutionary Movement in Georgia, 1763-1777*. Chicago, 1937.

12 MC CAUL, Robert L. "Education in Georgia During the Period of Royal Government, 1752-1776." *Ga Hist Q*, XL (1956), 103-112, 248-259.

13 REESE, Trevor R. *Colonial Georgia: A Study in British Imperial Policy in the Eighteenth Century*. Athens, Ga., 1963.

14 SAYE, Albert B. *New Viewpoints on Georgia History*. Athens, Ga., 1943.

15 STRICKLAND, Reba C. "The Mercantile System as Applied to Georgia." *Ga Hist Q*, XXII (1938), 160-168.

See also 16.1, 18.2, 24.16, 40.8, 98.1, 104.8.

4. The Frontier and the West

16 ABERNETHY, Thomas P. *From Frontier to Plantation in Tennessee: A Study in Frontier Democracy*. Chapel Hill, 1932.

1 ALVORD, Clarence W. *The Illinois Country, 1673-1818.* Vol. I of *The Centennial History of Illinois*, Springfield, Mass., 1920.

2 BARNHART, John D. *Valley of Democracy: The Frontier Versus the Plantation in the Ohio Valley, 1775-1818.* Bloomington, 1953.†

3 BAST, Homer. "Creek Indian Affairs, 1775-1778." *Ga Hist Q*, XXXIII (1949), 1-25.

4 BUSHNELL, David I., Jr. "The Virginia Frontier in History—1778." *Va Mag Hist*, XXIII (1915), 113-123, 256-268, 337-351.

5 CAUGHEY, John W. *Bernardo de Gálvez in Lousiana, 1776-1783.* Berkeley, 1934.

6 HACKETT, Charles W., G. P. HAMMOND, and J. L. MECHAM, eds. *New Spain and the Anglo-American West; Historical Contributions Presented to Herbert Eugene Bolton.* Vol. I. Los Angeles, 1932.

7 HENDERSON, Archibald. "The Creative Forces in American Expansion: Henderson and Boone." *Am Hist Rev*, XX (1914), 86-107.

8 HENDERSON, Archibald. "A Pre-Revolutionary Revolt in the Old Southwest." *Miss Val Hist Rev*, XVII (1930), 191-212.

9 JAMES, James A. "The Northwest: Gift or Conquest?" *Ind Mag Hist*, XXX (1934), 1-15.

10 JAMES, James A. *Oliver Pollock; The Life and Times of an Unknown Patriot.* New York, 1937.

11 JAMES, James A. "Spanish Influence in the West During the American Revolution." *Miss Val Hist Rev*, IV (1917), 193-208.

12 JAMES, James A. "To What Extent Was George Rogers Clark in Military Control of the Northwest at the Close of the American Revolution?" *Ann Rep Am Hist Assn, for the Year 1917.* Washington, D.C., 1920, pp. 313-329.

13 LAUB, C. Herbert. "The Problem of Armed Invasion of the Northwest During the American Revolution." *Va Mag Hist*, XLII (1934), 18-27, 132-144.

14 MASON, Kathryn Harrod. *James Harrod of Kentucky.* Baton Rouge, 1951.

15 MOOD, Fulmer. "Studies in the History of American Settled Areas and Frontier Lines: . . . 1625-1790." *Ag Hist*, XXVI (1952), 16-34.

16 NAVARRO LATORRE, José, and Fernando Solano COSTA. *Conspiración Española? 1787-1789.* Zaragoza, 1949.

17 PEASE, Theodore C. "1780—The Revolution at Crisis in the West." *J Ill St Hist Soc*, XXIII (1931), 664-681.

18 PHILBRICK, Francis S. *The Rise of the West, 1754-1830.* New York, 1965.†

19 PHILLIPS, Paul C. *The West in the Diplomacy of the American Revolution.* Urbana, Ill., 1913; repr. 1966.

20 SOSIN, Jack M. *The Revolutionary Frontier, 1763-1783.* New York, 1967.†

1 SWIGGETT, Howard. *War Out of Niagara; Walter Butler and the Tory Rangers.* New York, 1933.

2 VAN EVERY, Dale. *Ark of Empire: The American Frontier, 1784-1803.* New York, 1963.†

3 VAN EVERY, Dale. *A Company of Heroes: The American Frontier, 1775-1783.* New York, 1962.†

4 WILLIAMS, Samuel C. *Tennessee During the Revolutionary War.* Nashville, 1944.

5 WILSON, E. Lyon. *Louisiana in French Diplomacy, 1759-1804.* Norman, Okla., 1934.

6 WRIGHT, Louis B. *Culture on the Moving Frontier.* Bloomington, 1955.†

See also 14.5, 14.8, 36.13, 37.9, 43.3, 43.4.

5. The Nonrevolutionary Colonies

7 ARMSTRONG, Maurice W. "Neutrality and Religion in Revolutionary Nova Scotia." *N Eng Q*, XIX (1946), 50-62.

8 BARRS, Burton. *East Florida in the American Revolution.* Jacksonville, 1932.

9 BREBNER, John B. *The Neutral Yankees of Nova Scotia.* New York, 1937.†

10 BURT, Alfred L. *The Old Province of Quebec.* Minneapolis and Toronto, 1933.†

11 CALKIN, Homer L. "American Influence in Ireland, 1760-1800." *Pa Mag Hist*, LXXI (1947), 103-120.

12 COFFIN, Victor. "The Province of Quebec and the Early American Revolution: A Study in English-American Colonial History." *Bull Econ Pol Sci Hist Ser* (Wis), I (1896), 275-562.

13 COUPLAND, Reginald. *The American Revolution and the British Empire.* London, 1930.

14 CREIGHTON, Donald G. *The Empire of the St. Lawrence.* Toronto, 1956.

15 GRAHAM, Gerald S. *British Policy and Canada, 1774-1791: A Study in Eighteenth-Century Trade Policy.* London and New York, 1930.

16 HOFFMAN, Philip G. "Australia's Debt to the American Revolution." *Historian*, XVII (1955), 143-156.

17 HOWARD, Clinton N. *The British Development of West Florida, 1763-1769.* Berkeley and Los Angeles, 1947.

18 INNIS, Harold A. *The Fur Trade in Canada: An Introduction to Canadian Economic History.* London and New Haven, 1930.†

19 JOHNSON, Cecil. *British West Florida, 1763-1783.* London and New Haven, 1943.

1   KERR, Wilfred B. *Bermuda and the American Revolution, 1760-1783.* Princeton, 1936.

2   KERR, Wilfred B. *The Maritime Provinces of British North America and the American Revolution.* Sackville, Canada, 1941.

3   KERR, Wilfred B. "The Merchants of Nova Scotia and the American Revolution." *Canad Hist Rev*, XIII (1932), 20-36.

4   KERR, Wilfred B. "Newfoundland in the Period Before the American Revolution." *Pa Mag Hist*, LXV (1941), 56-78.

5   KRAUS, Michael. "America and the Irish Revolutionary Movement in the Eighteenth Century." In *Era of the American Revolution*, ed. Richard B. Morris. New York, 1939.

6   LANCTOT, Gustave. *Le Canada et la Révolution Américaine, 1774-1783.* Montreal, 1965.

7   MAKINSON, David H. *Barbados: A Study of North-American-West-Indian Relations, 1739-1789.* The Hague, 1964.

8   MARSHALL, Peter. "The British Empire and the American Revolution." *Hunt Lib Q*, XXVII (1964), 135-145.

9   MOWAT, Charles L. *East Florida as a British Province, 1763-1784.* Berkeley and Los Angeles, 1943.

10   MOYNE, Ernest J. "The Reverend William Hazlitt: A Friend of Liberty in Ireland During the American Revolution." *Wm Mar Q*, 3d ser., XXI (1964), 288-297.

11   PENNINGTON, Edgar L. "East Florida and the American Revolution, 1775-1778." *Fla Hist Q*, IX (1930), 24-46.

12   RICH, Edwin E. *Montreal and the Fur Trade.* Montreal, 1966.

13   ROBERTSON, E. A. *The Spanish Town Papers: Some Sidelights on the American War of Independence.* New York, 1959.

14   ROBINSON, Percy J. *Toronto During the French Régime: A History of the Toronto Region from Brûle to Simcoe, 1615-1793.* Toronto, 1965.†

15   SMITH, Justin H. *Our Struggle for the Fourteenth Colony.* New York, 1907.

16   STOCK, Leo F. "The Irish Parliament and the American Revolution." *U S Cath Hist Soc Rec*, XXX (1939), 11-29.

17   WRONG, George M. *Canada and the American Revolution.* New York, 1935.

See also 11.13, 14.10, 17.6, 17.13, 27.4, 28.5, 29.14, 33.6, 40.16, 40.17, 40.18, 41.14.

VII. Biographical Studies

1. Collective Biography

18   DEXTER, Franklin B. *Biographical Sketches of the Graduates of Yale College.* 6 vols. New York, 1885-1912.

1 EINSTEIN, Lewis. *Divided Loyalties: Americans in England During the War of Independence.* New York, 1948.

2 JOHNSON, Allen E., and Dumas MALONE, eds. *Dictionary of American Biography.* 20 vols. New York, 1928-1936.

3 NAMIER, Sir Lewis, and John BROOKE. *The History of Parliament: The House of Commons, 1754-1790.* 3 vols. New York, 1964.

4 ROSENBLOOM, Joseph R. *A Biographical Dictionary of Early American Jews, Colonial Times Through 1800.* Lexington, Ky., 1960.

5 SIBLEY, John L., and Clifford K. SHIPTON. *Sibley's Harvard Graduates.* 15 vols., in progress. Cambridge, Mass., 1873-1885, 1933- .

6 STEPHEN, Leslie, and Sydney LEE, eds. *Dictionary of National Biography.* 63 vols. London, 1885-1901.

7 WRAXALL, Nathaniel W. *Historical Memoirs of My Own Time: From 1772 to 1784.* 2 vols. London, 1815.

See also 84.16, 87.14, 100.2.

2. American Revolutionaries

(Alphabetically by subject)

8 BAILYN, Bernard. "Butterfield's Adams: Notes for a Sketch." *Wm Mar Q,* 3d ser., XIX (1962), 238-256.

9 BOWEN, Catherine Drinker. *John Adams and the American Revolution.* Boston, 1950.†

10 BUTTERFIELD, Lyman H., Wendell D. GARRETT, and Marjorie E. SPRAGUE, eds. *John Adams Family Correspondence.* 2 vols. Cambridge, Mass., 1963.†

11 BUTTERFIELD, Lyman H., et al., eds. *Diary and Autobiography of John Adams.* 4 vols. and supplement. Cambridge, Mass., 1961, 1966.†

12 CHINARD, Gilbert. *Honest John Adams.* Boston, 1933.†

13 ELLSWORTH, John W. "John Adams: The American Revolution as a Change of Heart?" *Hunt Lib Q,* XXVIII (1965), 293-300.

14 HARASZTI, Zoltan. *John Adams and the Prophets of Progress.* Cambridge, Mass., 1952.†

15 HOWE, John R., Jr. *The Changing Political Thought of John Adams.* Princeton, 1966.†

16 KURTZ, Stephen G. "The Political Science of John Adams, A Guide to His Statecraft." *Wm Mar Q,* 3d ser., XXV (1968), 605-613.

17 KURTZ, Stephen G. *The Presidency of John Adams: The Collapse of Federalism, 1795-1800.* Philadelphia, 1957.†

18 RIPLEY, R. B. "Adams, Burke, and Eighteenth Century Conservatism." *Pol Sci Q,* LXXX (1965), 216-235.

19 SMITH, Page. *John Adams, 1735-1826.* 2 vols. Garden City, N.Y., 1962.

On John Adams see also 78.13.

1 EAST, Robert A. *John Quincy Adams: The Critical Years, 1785-1794.* New York, 1962.

2 HARLOW, Ralph V. *Samuel Adams, Promoter of the American Revolution: A Study in Psychology and Politics.* New York, 1923.

3 JELLISON, Charles A. *Ethan Allen: Frontier Rebel.* Syracuse, 1969.

4 PELL, John H. G. *Ethan Allen.* Boston, 1929.

5 SHAPIRO, Darline. "Ethan Allen: Philosopher-Theologian to a Generation of American Revolutionaries." *Wm Mar Q,* 3d ser., XXI (1964), 236-255.

6 BERNHARD, Winfred E. A. *Fisher Ames: Federalist and Statesman, 1758-1808.* Chapel Hill, 1965.

7 WALLACE, Willard M. *Traitorous Hero: The Life and Fortunes of Benedict Arnold.* New York, 1954.

8 CANTOR, Milton. "Joel Barlow: Laywer and Legal Philosopher." *Am Q,* X (1958), 167-174.

9 DORFMAN, Joseph. "Joel Barlow: Trafficker in Trade and Letters." *Pol Sci Q,* LIX (1944), 83-100.

10 WOODRESS, James. *A Yankee's Odyssey: The Life of Joel Barlow.* Philadelphia, 1958.

11 KITE, Elizabeth S. *Beaumarchais and the War of Independence.* 2 vols. Boston, 1918.

12 CLARK, William B. *Captain Dauntless: The Story of Nicholas Biddle of the Continental Navy.* Baton Rouge, 1949.

13 KEITH, Alice B. "William Blount in North Carolina Politics, 1781-1789." In *Studies in Southern History,* ed. J. C. Sitterson. Chapel Hill, 1957.

14 MASTERSON, William H. *William Blount.* Baton Rouge, 1954.

15 BOYD, George A. *Elias Boudinot: Patriot and Statesman, 1740-1821.* Princeton, 1952.

16 WALETT, Francis G. "James Bowdoin, Patriot Propagandist." *N Eng Q,* XXIII (1950), 320-338.

17 WINTHROP, Robert C. *The Life and Services of James Bowdoin.* Boston, 1876.

18 NEWLIN, Claude M. *The Life and Writings of Hugh Henry Brackenridge.* Princeton, 1932.

19 THOMPSON, Mack. *Moses Brown: Reluctant Reformer.* Chapel Hill, 1962.

20 DOUGLASS, Elisha P. "Thomas Burke, Disillusioned Democrat." *N C Hist Rev,* XXVI (1949), 150-186.

21 SANDERS, Jennings B. "Thomas Burke in the Continental Congress." *N C Hist Rev,* IX (1932), 22-37.

22 SCHACHNER, Nathan. *Aaron Burr: A Biography.* New York, 1937.

1   ULMER, S. Sidney. "The Role of Pierce Butler in the Constitutional Convention." *Rev Pol*, XXII (1960), 361-374.

2   ROWLAND, Kate M. *Life of Charles Carroll*. 2 vols. New York, 1898.

3   SMITH, Ellen H. *Charles Carroll of Carrollton*. Cambridge, Mass., 1942.

4   MELVILLE, Annabelle M. *John Carroll of Baltimore, Founder of the American Catholic Hierarchy*. New York, 1955.

5   BERNHARD, Harold E. *Charles Chauncy: Colonial Liberal, 1705-1787*. Chicago, 1948.

6   BAKELESS, John E. *Background to Glory: The Life of George Rogers Clark*. Philadelphia, 1957.

7   JAMES, James A. *The Life of George Rogers Clark*. Chicago, 1928.

8   SPAULDING, Ernest W. *His Excellency George Clinton (1739-1812), Critic of the Constitution*. New York, 1938.

9   DESTLER, Chester M. *Joshua Coit: American Federalist, 1758-1798*. Middletown, Conn., 1962.

10 PROWN, Jules D. *John Singleton Copley*. 2 vols. Cambridge, Mass., 1966.

11 DAVIDSON, Chalmers. *Piedmont Partisan: The Life and Times of Brigadier-General William Lee Davidson*. Davidson, N.C., 1951.

12 ROBINSON, Blackwell P. *William R. Davie*. Chapel Hill, 1957.

13 ABERNETHY, Thomas P. "Commercial Activities of Silas Deane in France." *Am Hist Rev*, XXXIX (1934), 479-485.

14 BOYD, Julian P. "Silas Deane: Death by a Kindly Teacher of Treason?" *Wm Mar Q*, 3d ser., XVI (1959), 165-187, 319-342, 515-550.

15 CLARK, George L. *Silas Deane: A Connecticut Leader in the American Revolution*. London and New York, 1913.

16 COLBOURN, H. Trevor. "John Dickinson, Historical Revolutionary." *Pa Mag Hist*, LXXXIII (1959), 271-292.

17 JACOBSON, David L. *John Dickinson and the Revolution in Pennsylvania, 1764-1776*. Berkeley and Los Angeles, 1965.

18 STILLE, Charles J. *The Life and Times of John Dickinson, 1732-1808*. Philadelphia, 1891.

On John Dickinson, see also 78.13.

19 DABNEY, William M., and Marion DARGAN. *Williaam Henry Drayton and the American Revolution*. Albuquerque, 1962.

20 ALEXANDER, Edward P. *A Revolutionary Conservative: James Duane of New York*. New York, 1938.

21 KITE, Elizabeth S. *Brigadier-General Louis Lebègue Duportail, Commandant of Engineers in the Continental Army, 1779-1783*. Baltimore, 1933.

1 CUNNINGHAM, Charles E. *Timothy Dwight, 1752-1817.* New York, 1942.

2 SILVERMAN, Kenneth. *Timothy Dwight.* New York, 1969.

3 BROWN, William G. *Life of Oliver Ellsworth.* New York, 1905.

4 AIKEN, John R. "Benjamin Franklin, Karl Marx, and the Labor Theory of Value." *Pa Mag Hist*, XV (1966), 378-422.

5 BECKER, Carl L. *Benjamin Franklin: A Biographical Sketch.* Ithaca, N.Y., 1946. (First published in the *Dictionary of American Biography.* See 63.2.)

6 BUSHMAN, Richard L. "On the Uses of Psychology: Conflict and Conciliation in Benjamin Franklin." *Hist Theory*, V (1966), 225-240.

7 CONNOR, Paul W. *Poor Richard's Politicks: Benjamin Franklin and His New American Order.* New York, 1965.

8 CRANE, Verner W. *Benjamin Franklin and a Rising People.* Boston, 1954.†

9 GLEASON, J. Philip. "A Scurrilous Colonial Election and Franklin's Reputation." *Wm Mar Q*, 3d ser., XVIII (1961), 68-84.

10 HANNA, William S. *Benjamin Franklin and Pennsylvania Politics.* Stanford, 1964.

11 HUTSON, James H. "Benjamin Franklin and the Parliamentary Grant for 1758." *Wm Mar Q*, 3d ser., XXIII (1966), 575-595.

12 KETCHAM, Ralph L. *Benjamin Franklin.* New York, 1965.†

13 KORTY, Margaret B. *Benjamin Franklin and Eighteenth-Century American Libraries.* Philadelphia, 1965.

14 LABAREE, Leonard W. "Benjamin Franklin and the Defense of Pennsylvania, 1754-1757." *Pa Hist*, XXIX (1962), 7-23.

15 LABAREE, Leonard W. "Franklin and the Presbyterians." *J Presby Hist Soc*, XXXV (1957), 217-228.

16 LABAREE, Leonard W. "In Search of 'B. Franklin.'" *Wm Mar Q*, 3d ser., XVI (1959), 188-197.

17 LABAREE, Leonard W., et al. *The Papers of Benjamin Franklin.* 14 vols., in progress. New Haven, 1959- .

18 STOURZH, Gerald. *Benjamin Franklin and American Foreigh Policy.* Chicago, 1954.

19 VAN DOREN, Carl. *Benjamin Franklin.* New York, 1938.†

20 WEAVER, Glenn. "Benjamin Franklin and the Pennsylvania Germans." *Wm Mar Q*, 3d ser., XIV (1957), 536-559.

21 ZIMMERMAN, John J. "Benjamin Franklin and *The Pennsylvania Chronicle.*" *Pa Mag Hist*, LXXI (1957), 351-364.

On Benjamin Franklin, see also 26.15, 40.5, 97.3.

22 AXELRAD, Jacob. *Philip Freneau: Champion of Democracy.* Austin, 1967.

23 LEARY, Lewis G. *That Rascal Freneau: A Study in Literary Failure.* New Brunswick, 1941.

1   BILLIAS, George A. *John Glover and His Marblehead Mariners.* New York, 1960.

2   LEWIS, Charles L. *Admiral de Grasse and American Independence.* Baltimore, 1945.

3   GREENE, George W. *The Life of Nathanael Greene, Major-General in the Army of the Revolution.* 3 vols. New York, 1867-1871.

4   THAYER, Theodore. *Nathanael Greene: Strategist of the American Revolution.* New York, 1960.

5   ADAIR, Douglass, and Marvin HARVEY. "Was Alexander Hamilton a Christian Statesman?" *Wm Mar Q*, 3d ser., XII (1955), 308-329.

6   BEIN, Alex "Die Staatsidee Alexander Hamilton in ihrer Entstehung und Entwicklung." *Hist Zeit*, Beiheft 12 (1927).

7   COOKE, Jacob E. "Alexander Hamilton's Authorship of the 'Caesar' Letters." *Wm Mar Q*, 3d ser., XVII (1960), 78-85.

8   GOEBEL, Julius, et al., eds. *The Law Practice of Alexander Hamilton: Documents and Commentary.* Vol. I. New York, 1964.

9   GOVAN, Thomas P. "The Rich, the Well-Born, and Alexander Hamilton." *Miss Val Hist Rev*, XXXVI (1950), 675-680.

10 HACKER, Louis M. *Alexander Hamilton in the American Tradition.* New York, 1957.

11 MARSH, Philip M. "Hamilton's Neglected Essays, 1791-1793." *N-Y Hist Soc Q*, XXXII (1948), 280-300.

12 MEYER, Freeman W. "A Note on the Origins of the 'Hamiltonian System.'" *Wm Mar Q*, 3d ser., XXI (1964), 579-588.

13 MILLER, John C. *Alexander Hamilton: Portrait in Paradox.* New York, 1959.†

14 MITCHELL, Broadus. *Alexander Hamilton.* 2 vols. New York, 1957-1962.

15 NIX, Foster C. "Alexander Hamilton's Early Years in the American Colonies." *Wm Mar Q*, 3d ser., XXI (1964), 390-407.

16 PANAGOPOULOUS, E. P. "Hamilton's Notes in His Pay Book of the New York State Artillery Company." *Am Hist Rev*, LXII (1957), 310-325.

17 STOURZH, Gerald. *Alexander Hamilton and the Idea of Republican Government.* Stanford, 1970.

18 SYRETT, Harold C., and Jacob E. COOKE, eds. *The Papers of Alexander Hamilton.* 11 vols., in progress. London and New York, 1961- .

On Alexander Hamilton, see also 96.6, 110.8, 110.9.

19 ALLAN, Herbert S. *John Hancock: Patriot in Purple.* New York, 1948.

20 BAXTER, William T. *The House of Hancock, Business in Boston, 1724-1774.* Cambridge, Mass., 1945.

1 DICKERSON, Oliver M. "John Hancock: Notorious Smuggler or Near Victim of British Revenue Racketeers?" *Miss Val Hist Rev*, XXXII (1946), 515-540.

2 HENRY, William Wirt. *Patrick Henry: Life, Correspondence and Speeches.* 3 vols. Philadlephia, 1817; rev. ed., 1891.

3 MAYO, Bernard. *Myths and Men: Patrick Henry, George Washington, Thomas Jefferson.* Athens, Ga., 1959.

4 MEADE, Robert D. *Patrick Henry.* 2 vols. Philadelphia, 1957 and 1969.

5 FORBUSH, Bliss. *Elias Hicks: Quaker Liberal.* New York, 1956.

6 MC REE, Griffith J. *Life and Correspondence of James Iredell.* 2 vols. New York, 1857-1858.

7 MONAGHAN, Frank. *John Jay.* New York, 1935.

8 MORRIS, Richard B. "John Jay and the New England Connection." *Proc Mass Hist Soc*, LXXX (1968), 16-37.

9 MORRIS, Richard B. *John Jay, The Nation and the Court.* Boston, 1967.

10 BOYD, Julian P. "The Megalonyx, the Megatherium, and Thomas Jefferson's Lapse of Memory." *Proc Am Philos Soc*, CII (1958), 420-435.

11 BOYD, Julian P. "Thomas Jefferson and the Police State." *N C Hist Rev*, XXV (1948), 233-253.

12 BOYD, Julian P., et al. *The Papers of Thomas Jefferson.* 17 vols., in progress. Princeton, 1950- .

13 CHINARD, Gilbert. *Thomas Jefferson: The Apostle of Americanism.* Rev. ed. Ann Arbor, 1957.

14 COLBOURN, H. Trevor. "Thomas Jefferson's Use of the Past." *Wm Mar Q*, 3d ser., CV (1958), 56-70.

15 KAPLAN, Lawrence. S. *Jefferson and France: An Essay on Politics and Political Ideas.* New Haven, 1967.

16 KIMBALL, Marie. *Jefferson.* 3 vols. New York, 1943-1950.

17 MALONE, Dumas. *Jefferson and His Time.* 4 vols., in progress. Boston, 1948- .†

18 MALONE, Dumas. *Thomas Jefferson as Political Leader.* Berkeley, 1963.

19 PALMER, Robert R. "The Dubious Democrat: Thomas Jefferson in Bourbon France." *Pol Sci Q*, LXXII (1957), 388-404.

20 PALMER, Robert R. "A Neglected Work: Otto Vossler on Jefferson and the Revolutionary Era." *Wm Mar Q*, 3d ser., XII (1955), 462-471.

21 PETERSON, Merrill D. *Thomas Jefferson and the New Nation.* New York, 1970.

On Thomas Jefferson, see also 80.4, 111.3.

1 GROCE, George C. *William Samuel Johnson: A Maker of the Constitution.* New York, 1937.

2 MORISON, Samuel E. *John Paul Jones: A Sailor's Biography.* Boston, 1959.†

3 ZUCKER, A. E. *General De Kalb, Lafayette's Mentor.* Chapel Hill, 1966.

4 KAPP, Friedrich. *Life of John Kalb.* New York, 1870.

5 ERNST, Robert. *Rufus King: American Federalist.* Chapel Hill, 1968.

6 CALLAHAN, North. *Henry Knox: General Washington's General.* New York, 1958.

7 HAIMAN, Miecislaus. *Kosciuszko in the American Revolution.* New York, 1943.

8 GOTTSCHALK, Louis. *Lafayette* . . . . 5 vols., in progress. Chicago, 1935-1969.

9 MATHIEZ, Albert. "Lafayette et le Commerce Franco-Américaine à la Veille de la Révolution [Française]." *Annales Historiques de la Révolution Française,* n.s., III (1926), 474-484.

10 LEAKE, Issac Q. *Memoir of the Life and Times of General John Lamb.* Albany, 1850.

11 HARMER, Philip M. "Henry Laurens of South Carolina—The Man and His Papers." *Proc Mass Hist Soc,* LXXVII (1965), 3-14.

12 WALLACE, David D. *The Life of Henry Laurens: With a Sketch of the Life of Lieutenant-Colonel John Laurens.* London and New York, 1915.

13 TOWNSEND, Sara B. *An American Soldier: The Life of John Laurens* . . . . Raleigh, 1958.

14 ALDEN, John R. *General Charles Lee, Traitor or Patriot?* Baton Rouge, 1951.

15 CHITWOOD, Oliver Perry. *Richard Henry Lee, Statesman of the Revolution.* Morgantown, W. Va., 1968.

16 DANGERFIELD, George. *Chancellor Robert R. Livingston of New York, 1746-1813.* New York, 1960.

17 SEDGWICK, Theodore, Jr. *A Memoir of the Life of William Livingston.* New York, 1833.

18 TOLLES, Frederick B. *George Logan of Philadelphia.* New York, 1953.

19 LAWRENCE, Alexander A. "General Lachlan McIntosh and His Suspension from Continental Command During the Revolution." *Ga Hist Q,* XXXVIII (1954), 101-141.

20 BRANT, Irving. *James Madison.* 6 vols. Indianapolis, 1941-1961. On James Madison, see also 96.9, 97.1, 108.1, 111.14.

21 BASS, Robert D. *Swamp Fox: The Life and Campaigns of General Francis Marion.* New York, 1959.

1 JAMES, William D. *A Sketch of the Life of Brig. Gen. Francis Marion . . . .* Charleston, 1821; repr. Marietta, Ga., 1948.

2 BEVERIDGE, Albert J. *The Life of John Marshall.* 4 vols. Boston, 1916-1919.

3 MORISON, Samuel E. "The Education of John Marshall." *Atlantic*, CXXVI (1920), 45-54.

4 ROWLAND, Kate M. *Life of George Mason.* 2 vols. New York, 1892.

5 RUTLAND, Robert A. *George Mason: Reluctant Statesman.* Williamsburg, 1961.†

6 AKERS, Charles W. *Called unto Liberty: A Life of Jonathan Mayhew, 1720-1766.* Cambridge, Mass., 1964.

7 ROSSMAN, Kenneth R. *Thomas Mifflin and the Politics of the American Revolution.* Chapel Hill, 1952.

8 CRESSON, William P. *James Monroe.* Chapel Hill, 1946.

9 HIGGINBOTHAM, Don. *Daniel Morgan: Revolutionary Rifleman.* Chapel Hill, 1961.

10 BELL, Whitfield J. Jr. *John Morgan: Continental Doctor.* Philadelphia, 1965.

11 VER STEEG, Clarence L. *Robert Morris, Revolutionary Financier: With an Analysis of His Earlier Career.* Philadelphia, 1954.

12 TUDOR, William. *The Life of James Otis of Massachusetts; Containing Also Notices of Some Contemporary Characters and Events from the Year 1760 to 1775.* Boston, 1823. See 12.2.

13 ALDRIDGE, Alfred O. "Some Writings of Thomas Paine in Pennsylvania Newspapers." *Am Hist Rev*, LVI (1951), 732-838.

14 ALDRIDGE, Alfred O. "Thomas Paine and Comus." *Pa Mag Hist*, LXXXV (1961), 70-75.

15 CLARK, Harry H. "Toward a Reinterpretation of Thomas Paine." *Am Lit*, V (1933), 133-145.

16 CONWAY, Moncure D. *Life of Thomas Paine.* 2 vols. New York, 1892.

17 PALMER, Robert R. "Tom Paine: Victim of the Rights of Man." *Pa Mag Hist*, LXVI (1942), 161-175.

On Thomas Paine, see also 96.7.

18 BELL, Whitfield J., Jr. "Thomas Parke, M.B.: Physician and Friend." *Wm Mar Q*, 3d ser., VI (1949), 569-595.

19 SELLERS, Charles C. *Charles Willson Peale.* 2 vols. Philadelphia, 1947.

20 WARING, Alice Noble. *The Fighting Elder: Andrew Pickens (1739-1817).* Columbia, S.C., 1962.

21 UPHAM, C.W. *Life of Timothy Pickering.* Boston, 1873.

1 ULMER, S. Sidney. "Charles Pinckney: Father of the Constitution?" *S C Law Q*, X (1958), 225-247.

2 ZAHNISER, Marvin R. *Charles Cotesworth Pinckney: Founding Father.* Chapel Hill, 1967.

3 PINCKNEY, Charles C. *The Life of General Thomas Pinckney.* Boston, 1895.

4 PINKNEY, William. *The Life of William Pinkney.* New York, 1853; repr. 1969.

5 TURNER, Lynn W. *William Plumer of New Hampshire, 1759-1850.* Chapel Hill, 1962.

6 GORDON, William W. "Count Casimir Pulaski." *Ga Hist Q*, XIII (1929), 167-227.

7 QUINCY, Josiah. *Memoir of the Life of Josiah Quincy, Junior.* 3d ed. Boston, 1875.

8 BRANT, Irving. "Edmund Randolph, Not Guilty." *Wm Mar Q*, 3d ser., VII (1950), 179-198.

9 READ, William T. *Life and Correspondence of George Read.* Philadelphia, 1870.

10 REED, William B. *Life and Correspondence of Joseph Reed.* 2 vols. Philadelphia, 1847.

11 ROCHE, John F. *Joseph Reed: A Moderate in the American Revolution.* New York, 1957.

12 FORBES, Esther. *Paul Revere and the World He Lived In.* Boston, 1942.†

13 HINDLE, Brooke. *David Rittenhouse.* Princeton, 1964.

14 WEELEN, Jean E. *Rochambeau.* Paris, 1934.

15 LAINE, E. "Rochambeau. A propos d'un volume récent." *Revue des Etudes Historiques*, CII (1935), 66-77. (On Wheelen.)

16 WHITRIDGE, Arnold. "The Marquis de la Rouërie, Brigadier Generalin the Continental Army." *Proc Mass Hist Soc*, LXXIX (1967), 47-63.

17 BUTTERFIELD, Lyman H. "The Reputation of Benjamin Rush." *Pa Hist*, XVII (1950), 3-22.

18 GOODMAN, Nathan G. *Benjamin Rush, Physician and Citizen, 1746-1813.* Philadelphia, 1934.

On Benjamin Rush, see also 98.4.

19 BARRY, Richard H. *Mr. [John] Rutledge of South Carolina.* New York, 1942.

20 GERLACH, Don R. *Philip Schuyler and the American Revolution in New York, 1733-1777.* Lincoln, Neb., 1964.

21 TUCKERMAN, Bayard. *Life of General Philip Schuyler, 1733-1804.* New York, 1903.

1   WELCH, Richard E. *Theodore Sedgwick, Federalist: A Political Portrait.* Middletown, Conn., 1965.

2   DRIVER, Carl S. *John Sevier, Pioneer of the Old Southwest.* Chapel Hill, 1932.

3   BOARDMAN, Roger S. *Roger Sherman, Signer and Statesman.* Philadelphia, 1938.

4   ROGERS, George C., Jr. *Evolution of a Federalist: William Loughton Smith of Charleston (1758-1812).* Columbia, S.C., 1962.

5   KAPP, Friedrich. *Life of Major General Frederick William von Steuben.* New York, 1859.

6   PALMER, John M. *General von Steuben.* New Haven, 1937.

7   MORGAN, Edmund S. *The Gentle Puritan: A Life of Ezra Stiles, 1727-1795.* New Haven, 1962.

8   WHITTEMORE, Charles P. *A General of the Revolution: John Sullivan of New Hampshire.* New York, 1961.

9   GREGORIE, Anna K. *Thomas Sumter.* Columbia, S.C., 1931.

10   HALL, Charles S. *Benjamin Tallmadge: Revolutionary Soldier and Statesman.* New York, 1943.

11   ZIMMERMAN, John J. "Charles Thomson, 'The Sam Adams of Philadelphia.'" *Miss Val Hist Rev*, XLV (1958), 464-480.

12   FERGUSON, Eugene S. *Truxtun of the Constellation: The Life of Commodore Thomas Truxton, U.S. Navy, 1755-1822.* Baltimore, 1956.

13   MONTMORT, Roger, Comte de. *Antoine Charles du Houx, Baron de Vioménil, Lieutenant-General of the Armies of the King, Second in Command Under Rochambeau.* Baltimore, 1935.

14   CARY, John. *Joseph Warren: Physician, Politician, Patriot.* Urbana, Ill., 1961.

15   CUNLIFFE, Marcus. *George Washington: Man and Monument.* Boston, 1957.†

16   FLEXNER, James T. *George Washington.* 2 vols., in progress. Boston, 1965- .

17   FREEMAN, Douglas Southall. *George Washington: A Biography.* 7 vols. Vol. VII by John A. Carroll and Mary Wells Ashworth. New York, 1948-1957.

18   FROTHINGHAM, Thomas G. *Washington, Commander in Chief.* Boston and New York, 1930.

19   KNOLLENBERG, Bernhard. *George Washington: The Virginia Period, 1732-1775.* Durham, N.C., 1964.

20   MC GRANE, Reginald Charles. "George Washington as an Anglo-American Hero." *Va Mag Hist*, LXIII (1955), 3-14.

21   SPAULDING, Oliver L., Jr. "The Military Studies of George Washington." *Am Hist Rev*, XXIX (1924), 675-680.

1 STEPHENSON, Nathaniel W., and Waldo H. DUNN. *George Washington.* 2 vols. London and New York, 1940.

2 WEEMS, Mason L. *The Life of Washington*, ed Marcus Cunliffe. Cambridge, Mass., 1962.†

3 WRIGHT, Esmond. *Washington and the American Revolution.* New York, 1957.

On George Washington, see also 79.1, 80.2, 87.13, 88.10, 100.17.

4 WILDES, Harry E. *Anthony Wayne: A Trouble Shooter of the American Revolution.* New York, 1941.

5 CLARK, William B. *Lambert Wickes, Sea Raider and Diplomat.* New Haven, 1932.

6 HAY, Thomas R. "Some Reflections on the Career of General James Wilkinson." *Miss Val Hist Rev*, XXI (1935), 471-494.

7 JACOBS, James R. *Tarnished Warrior: Major-General James Wilkinson.* New York, 1938.

8 WILKINSON, James. *Memoirs of My Own Times.* 2 vols. Philadelphia, 1816.

9 LEAVELLE, Arnaud B. "James Wilson and the Relation of the Scottish Metaphysics to American Political Thought." *Pol Sci Q*, LVII (1942), 394-410.

10 SEED, Geoffrey. "The Democratic Ideas of James Wilson: A Reappraisal." *Bull Brit Assn Am Stud*, n.s., No. 10 (1965), 3-30.

11 SMITH, Charles Page. *James Wilson: Founding Father, 1742-1798.* Chapel Hill, 1956.

12 DANIEL, Marjorie. "John Joachim Zubly—Georgia Pamphleteer of the Revolution." *Ga Hist Q*, XIX (1935), 1-16.

3. Loyalists and Englishmen

(Alphabetically by subject)

13 WHITWORTH, Rex. "Field-Marshal Lord Amherst: A Military Enigma." With a reply by J. H. Broomfield. *Hist Today*, IX (1959), 132-137, 532.

14 BARRINGTON, Shute. *The Political Life of William Wildman, Viscount Barrington: Compiled from Original Papers.* London, 1815.

15 LUCAS, Paul. "Blackstone and the Reform of the Legal Profession." *Eng Hist Rev*, LXXVII (1962), 456-489.

16 LITTLE, Bryan. "Norbonne Berkeley [Lord Botetourt] Gloucestershire Magnate." *Va Mag Hist*, LXIII (1955), 379-409.

17 BOUCHIER, Jonathan, ed. *Reminiscences of an American Loyalist, 1738-1789: Being the Autobiography of the Rev. Jonathan Boucher.* Boston, 1925.

18 CLARK, Michael D. "Jonathan Boucher: The Mirror of Reaction." *Hunt Lib Q*, XXXIII (1969), 19-32.

1 WALKER, Robert G. "Jonathan Boucher: Champion of the Minority." *Wm Mar Q*, 3d ser., II (1945), 3-14.

2 HANDLIN, Oscar and Mary. "James Burgh and American Revolutionary Theory." *Proc Mass Hist Soc*, LXXIII (1961), 38-56.

3 DE FONBLANQUE, Edward B. *Political and Military Episodes . . . from the Life and Correspondence of the Rt. Hon. John Burgoyne.* London, 1876.

4 FOX, Dixon R. "Burgoyne, Before and After Saratoga." *J N Y St Hist Assn*, X (1929), 128-137.

5 HUDLESTON, F. J. *Gentleman Johnny Burgoyne.* London, 1928.

7 BROOKE, John. "Burke in the 1760s." *S Atl Q*, LXIII (1959), 548-555.

8 CONE, Carl B. *The Age of the American Revolution.* Vol. I of *Burke and the Nature of Politics.* Lexington, Ky., 1957.

9 COPELAND, Thomas W. "The Reputation of Edmund Burke." *J Brit Stud*, I (1961), 78-90.

10 HOFFMAN, Ross J. S., ed. *Edmund Burke, New York Agent, with His Letters to the New York Assembly and Intimate Correspondence with Charles O'Hara, 1761-1776.* Philadelphia, 1956.

11 MAHONEY, Thomas H. D. "Edmund Burke and the American Revolution: The Repeal of the Stamp Act." *Burke Newsletter*, XIII (1965-1966), 503-521.

12 SUTHERLAND, Lucy. "Edmund Burke and the First Rockingham Ministry." *Eng Hist Rev*, LXVIII (1932), 46-72.

13 UNDERDOWN, P. T. "Edmund Burke, the Commissary of His Bristol Constituents, 1774-1780." *Eng Hist Rev*, XVVIII (1958), 252-269.

14 BURT, A. L. *Guy Carleton, Lord Dorchester, 1724-1818: Revised Version.* Ottawa, 1955.

15 ROWLAND, Mrs. Dunbar. "Peter Chester: Third Governor of the Province of British West Florida Under British Dominion, 1770-1781." *Pub Miss Hist Soc*, V (1925), 1-183.

16 WILLCOX, William B. *Portrait of a General: Sir Henry Clinton in the War of Independence.* New York, 1964.

17 WILLCOX, William B., and Frederick WYATT. "Sir Henry Clinton: A Psychological Exploration in History." *Wm Mar Q*, 3d ser., XVI (1959), 3-26.

18 SHAMMAS, Carole. "Cadwallader Colden and the Role of the King's Prerogative." *N-Y Hist Soc Q*, LIII (1959), 103-126.

19 WICKWIRE, Franklin and Mary. *Cornwallis: The American Adventure.* Boston, 1970.

20 BARGAR, B. D. *Lord Dartmouth and the American Revolution.* Columbia, S.C., 1965.

1   LAND, Aubrey C. *The Dulanys of Maryland: A Biographical Study of Daniel Dulany the Elder (1685-1753) and Daniel Dulany the Younger (1772-1797).* Baltimore, 1955.

2   QUARLES, Benjamin. "Lord Dunmore as Liberator." *Wm Mar Q*, 3d ser., XV (1958), 494-507.

3   RAAB, Reginald E. "The Role of William Eden in the British Peace Commission of 1778." *Historian* XX (1958), 153-178.

4   FENELLY, Catherine. "William Franklin of New Jersey." *Wm Mar Q*, 3d ser., VI (1959), 361-382.

5   ALDEN, John R. *General Gage in America: Being Principally a History of His Role in the American Revolution.* Baton Rouge, 1948.

6   BALDWIN, Ernest H. "Joseph Galloway, the Loyalist Politician." *Pa Mag Hist*, XXVI (1902), 161-191, 289-321, 417-442.

7   BOYD, Julian P. *Anglo-American Union: Joseph Galloway's Plans to Preserve the British Empire, 1774-1788.* Philadelphia, 1941.

8   BERKELEY, Edmund, and Dorothy SMITH. *Dr. Alexander Garden of Charles Town.* Chapel Hill, 1969.

9   BROWN, Gerald S. *The American Secretary: The Colonial Policy of Lord George Germain, 1775-1778.* Ann Arbor, 1963.

10 VALENTINE, Alan C. *Lord George Germain.* Oxford, 1962.

11 BUTTERFIELD, Herbert. *George III and the Historians.* London, 1957.

12 BUTTERFIELD, Herbert. *George III, Lord North, and the People, 1779-1780.* London, 1949.

13 BUTTERFIELD, Herbert. "Some Reflections on the Early Years of George III's Reign." *J Brit Stud*, IV (1965), 78-101.

14 FRYER, W. R. "King George III: His Political Character and Conduct: 1760-1784: A New Whig Interpretation." *Ren Mod Stud*, VI (1962), 68-101.

15 MAC ALPINE, Ida, and Richard HUNTER. *George III and the Mad-Business.* London, 1969.

16 PARES, Richard. *George III and the Politicians.* Oxford, 1953.†

17 WIGGIN, Lewis M. *The Faction of Cousins: A Political Account of the Grenvilles, 1733-1763.* New Haven, 1958.

18 GUTTRIDGE, G. H. *David Hartley M.P.: An Advocate of Conciliation, 1774-1783.* Berkeley, 1926.

19 ANDERSON, Troyer S. *The Command of the Howe Brothers During the American Revolution.* London and New York, 1936. See also 85.11, 85.14.

20 FREIBERG, Malcolm. "How to Become a Colonial Governor: Thomas Hutchinson of Massachusetts." *Rev Pol*, XXI (1959), 646-656.

1 FREIBERG, Malcolm. "Prelude to Purgatory: Thomas Hutchinson in Provincial Massachusetts Politics, 1760-1770." Unpublished Ph.D. thesis, Brown U, 1951.

2 HOSMER, James K. *Life of Thomas Hutchinson, Royal Governor of the Province of Massachusetts Bay.* Boston, 1896.

3 SHIPTON, Clifford K. "Thomas Hutchinson." *Sibley's Harvard Graduates,* VIII (1951), 149-217.

4 GIPSON, Lawrence H. *Jared Ingersoll: A Study of American Loyalism in Relation to British Colonial Government.* New Haven, 1920.

5 WALKER, Mabel Gregory. "Sir John Johnson, Loyalist." *Miss Val Hist Rev,* III (1916), 318-346.

On Sir William Johnson, see 44.2.

6 MAC LEAN, J. N. *Reward is Secondary: The Life of a Political Adventurer and an Inquiry into the Mystery of "Junius."* London, 1963.

7 SUTHERLAND, Lucy S., W. DOYLE, and J. M. J. ROGISTER. "Junius and Philip Francis: New Evidence." *Bull Inst Hist Res,* XLII (1969), 158-172.

8 JACKMAN, Sydney W. "Daniel Leonard, 1740-1829." *Bermuda Hist Q,* XIII (1956), 136-145.

9 BECKWITH, Mildred C. "Catharine Macaulay: Eighteenth-Century Rebel." *Proc S C Hist Assn* (1958), 12-29.

10 DONNELLY, Lucy M. "The Celebrated Mrs. Macaulay." *Wm Mar Q,* 3d ser., VI (1949), 173-207.

11 LUCAS, Reginald. *Lord North, Second Earl of Guilford, K.G., 1732-1792.* 2 vols. London, 1913.

12 HOTBLACK, Kate. *Chatham's Colonial Policy: A Study in the Fiscal and Economic Implications of the Colonial Policy of the Elder Pitt.* London and New York, 1917.

13 RITCHESON, Charles R. "The Elder Pitt and an American Department." *Am Hist Rev,* LVII (1952), 376-383.

14 ROBERTSON, Charles G. *Chatham [William Pitt] and the British Empire.* London, 1946.†

15 RUVILLE, Albert von. *William Pitt, Graf von Chatham.* 3 vols. Trans H. J. Chaytor and M. Morrison. Stuttgart, 1905; London and New York, 1907.

16 SHERRARD, Owen A. *Lord Chatham [William Pitt] and America.* London, 1958.

17 WICKWIRE, Franklin B. "John Pownall and British Colonial Policy." *Wm Mar Q,* 3d ser., XX (1963), 543-554.

18 GUTTRIDGE, G. H. "Thomas Pownall's *The Administration of the Colonies:* The Six Editions." *Wm Mar Q,* 3d ser., XXVI (1969), 31-46.

1 SCHUTZ, John A. *Thomas Pownall, British Defender of American Liberty: A Study of Anglo-American Relations in the Eighteenth Century.* Glendale, Calif., 1951. See 33.15.

2 CONE, Carl B. *Torchbearer of Freedom: The Influence of Richard Price on Eighteenth-Century Thought.* Lexington, Ky., 1952.

3 OLSON, Alison G. *The Radical Duke: Career and Correspondence of Charles Lennox, Third Duke of Richmond.* Oxford, 1961.

4 KEPPEL, George Thomas, Earl of Albemarle. *Memoirs of the Marquis of Rockingham and His Contemporaries.* 2 vols. London, 1852.

5 CUNEO, John R. *Robert Rogers of the Rangers.* New York, 1959.

6 BROOMFIELD, J. H. "Lord Sandwich at the Admiralty Board: Politics and the British Navy, 1771-1778." *Mariner's Mirror*, LI (1954), 7-17.

7 THOMAS, Herbert. *Samuel Seabury: Priest and Physician, Bishop of Connecticut.* Hamden, Conn., 1963.

8 HUMPHREYS, R. A. "Lord Shelburne and a Projected Recall of Colonial Governors in 1767." *Am Hist Rev*, XXXVII (1932), 269-272.

9 HUMPHREYS, R. A. "Lord Shelburne and British Colonial Policy, 1766-1768." *Eng Hist Rev*, L (1935), 257-277.

10 NORRIS, John M. *Shelburne and Reform.* London and New York, 1963.

11 SUTHERLAND, Lucy S. "Lord Shelburne and East India Company Politics, 1766-9." *Eng Hist Rev*, XLIX (1934), 450-486.

12 CALHOON, Robert M. "William Smith, Jr.'s Alternative to the American Revolution." *Wm Mar Q*, 3d ser., XXII (1965), 105-118.

13 UPTON, L. F. S. *The Loyal Whig: William Smith of New York and Quebec.* Toronto, 1969.

14 BASS, Robert D. *The Green Dragoon: The Lives of Banastre Tarleton and Mary Robinson.* New York, 1957.

15 NAMIER, Sir Lewis, and John BROOKE. *Charles Townshend.* London and New York, 1964.

16 HAYWOOD, Marshall D. *Governor William Tryon and His Administration in the Province of North Carolina, 1765-1771.* Raleigh, 1903.

17 DILL, Alonzo T. *Governor Tryon and His Palace.* Chapel Hill, 1955.

18 MAYO, Lawrence S. *John Wentworth: Governor of New Hampshire, 1767-1775.* Cambridge, Mass., 1921.

19 HOLLAND, Lynwood M. "John Wesley and the American Revolution." *J Ch St*, V (1963), 199-213.

20 WALLACE, Willard M. "John Wesley and the American Revolution." In *Essays in Honor of Conyers Read*, ed Norton Downs. Chicago, 1953.

VIII. Revolutionary War

1 ALDEN, John R. *The American Revolution, 1775-1783.* New York, 1954.†

2 BELCHER, Henry. *The First American Civil War; First Period, 1775-1778. . . .* 2 vols. London, 1911.

1. The Political Economy of Revolutionary War

A. THE DECLARATION OF INDEPENDENCE

3 ADAMS, Thomas R. *American Independence: The Growth of an Idea.* Providence, 1965. (Bibliography.) See 1.1.

4 BECKER, Carl L. *The Declaration of Independence: A Study in the History of Political Ideas.* New York, 1922.

5 BOYD, Julian P. *The Declaration of Independence: The Evolution of the Text. . . .* Princeton, 1945.

6 CHAMPAGNE, Roger. "New York Politics and Independence, 1776." *N-Y Hist Soc Q*, XLVI (1962), 281-303.

7 EDMONDS, John H. "How Massachusetts Received the Declaration of Independence." *Proc Am Ant Soc*, n.s., XXXV (1926), 227-252.

8 FORCE, Peter, comp. *American Archives: Consisting of a Collection of Authentick Records, State Papers, Debates, and Letters and Other Notices of Publick Affairs . . . [1774-1776].* 9 vols. Washington, D.C., 1837-1853.

9 HAWKE, David. *A Transaction of Free Men: The Birth and Course of the Declaration of Independence.* New York, 1964.

10 HEAD, John M. *A Time to Rend: An Essay on the Decision for American Independence.* Madison, 1968.

11 HOWELL, Wilbur S. "The Declaration of Independence and Eighteenth-Century Logic." *Wm Mar Q*, 3d ser., XVIII (1961), 463-484.

12 KLINGELHOFER, Herbert E. "The Cautious Revolution: Maryland and the Movement Toward Independence: 1774-1776." *Md Hist Mag*, LX (1965), 261-313.

13 KNOLLENBERG, Bernhard. "John Dickinson vs. John Adams, 1774-1776." *Proc Am Philos Soc*, CVII (1963), 138-144.

14 MORISON, Samuel E. "Prelude to Independence: The Virginia Resolutions of May 15, 1776." *Wm Mar Q*, 3d ser., VIII (1951), 483-492.

1 NETTELS, Curtis P. *George Washington and American Independence.* Boston, 1951.

2 NETTELS, Curtis P. "A Link in the Chain of Events Leading to American Independence." *Wm Mar Q*, 3d ser., III (1946), 36-47.

3 WALL, Alexander J. "New York and the Declaration of Independence." *Bull N-Y Hist Soc*, X (1926), 43-51.

4 WOLF, Edwin, II. "Authorship of the 1774 Address to the King Restudied." *Wm Mar Q*, 3d ser., XXII (1965), 189-224.

B. THE POLITICS OF CONFEDERATION

5 BURNETT, Edmund C. *The Continental Congress.* New York, 1941.†

6 BURNETT, Edmund C., ed. *Letters of Members of the Continental Congress.* 8 vols. Washington, D.C., 1921-1936.

7 CAMPBELL, Randolph B. "The Case of the 'Three Friends': An Incident in Maritime Regulation During the Revolutionary War." *Va Mag Hist*, LXXIV (1966), 190-209.

8 COLLINS, Edward D. "Committees of Correspondence of the American Revolution." *An Rep Am Hist Assn*, I (1901), 243-271.

9 DABNEY, William M. "Drayton and Laurens in the Continental Congress." *S C Hist Mag*, LX (1959), 74-82.

10 DAVIS, Andrew M. "The Trials of a Governor in the Revolution." *Proc Mass Hist Soc*, LXVII (1914), 131-141.

11 GARVER, Frank H. "The Transition from the Continental Congress to the Congress of the Confederation." *Pac Hist Rev*, I (1932), 221-234.

12 GERLACH, Larry R. "A Delegation of Steady Habits: The Connecticut Representatives to the Continental Congress, 1774-1789." *Bull Conn Hist Soc*, XXXII (1967), 33-39.

13 GERLACH, Larry R. "Firmness and Prudence: Connecticut, the Continental Congress, and the National Domain, 1776-1786." *Bull Conn Hist Soc*, XXXI (1966), 65-75.

14 GIBSON, James E. "The Pennsylvania Provincial Conference of 1776." *Pa Mag Hist*, LVIII (1934), 312-341.

15 HENDERSON, H. James, Jr. "Congressional Factionalism and the Attempt to Recall Benjamin Franklin." *Wm Mar Q*, 3d ser., XXVII (1970), 246-267.

16 HENDERSON, H. James, Jr. "Political Factions in the Continental Congress, 1774-1783." Ph.D. thesis, Columbia University, 1962.

17 JENSEN, Merrill. *The Articles of Confederation: An Interpretation of the Social-Constitutional History of the American Revolution, 1774-1781.* Madison, 1948.†

1   JENSEN, Merrill. "The Idea of a National Government During the American Revolution." *Pol Sci Q*, LVIII (1943), 356-379.

2   KNOLLENBERG, Bernhard. *Washington and the Revolution, a Reappraisal: Gates, Conway, and the Continental Congress.* New York, 1940.

3   LAWSON, Murray G. "Canada and the Articles of Confederation." *Am Hist Rev*, LVIII (1952), 39-54.

4   LEWIS, Anthony M. "Jefferson's *Summary View* as a Chart of Political Union." *Wm Mar Q*, 3d ser., V (1948), 35-41.

5   MACMILLAN, Margaret B. *The War Governors in the American Revolution.* New York, 1943.

6   MEIGS, Cornelia L. *The Violent Men: A Study of Human Relations in the First American Congress [1774-76].* New York, 1949.

7   MONTROSS, Lynn. *The Reluctant Rebels: The Story of the Continental Congress, 1774-1789.* New York, 1950; repr. 1970.

8   MUNROE, John A. "Nonresident Representation in the Continental Congress: The Delaware Delegation of 1782." *Wm Mar Q*, 3d ser., IX (1952), 166-190.

9   NEVINS, Alan. *The American States During and After the Revolution, 1775-1789.* New York, 1924.

10   SANDERS, Jennings B. *Evolution of Executive Departments of the Continental Congress, 1774-1789.* Chapel Hill, 1935.

11   TAYLOR, Robert J. "Trial at Trenton." *Wm Mar Q*, 3d ser., XXVI (1969), 521-547.

12   *Warren-Adams Letters, Being Chiefly a Correspondence Among John Adams, Samuel Adams, and James Warren. Coll Mass Hist Soc*, v., LXXLL (1916).

C. THE MOBILIZATION OF SOCIETY

13   ALEXANDER, Arthur J. "Exemptions from Military Service in the Old Dominion During the War of the Revolution." *Va Mag Hist Biog*, LIII (1945), 163-171.

14   ALEXANDER, Arthur J. "Exemptions from Militia Service in New York State During the Revolutionary War." *N Y Hist*, XXVII (1946), 204-212.

15   ALEXANDER, Arthur J. "How Maryland Tried to Raise Her Continental Quotas." *Md Hist Mag*, XIII (1947), 184-196.

16   ALEXANDER, Arthur J. "Pennsylvania's Revolutionary Militia." *Pa Mag Hist*, LXIX (1945), 15-25.

17   ALEXANDER, Arthur J. "Service by Substitute in the Militia of Lancaster and Northampton Counties (Pennsylvania) During the War of the Revolution." *Mil Affairs*, IX (1945), 278-282.

18   ANDERSON, John R. "Militia Law in Colonial New Jersey." *Proc N J Hist Soc*, LXXVI (1958), 280-296; LXXVII (1959), 9-21.

19   BEHRENS, Kathryn L. "Paper Money in Maryland, 1727-1789." *Stud Hist Pol Sci* (Hop), 41st ser., (1934), 1-98.

1 BEZANSON, Anne. "Inflation and Controls, Pennsylvania, 1774-1779." *J Econ Hist*, VIII, supp. (1948), 1-20.

2 BURNETT, Edmund C. "The Continental Congress and Agricultural Supplies." *Ag Hist*, II (1928), 111-128.

3 COMETTI, Elizabeth. "The Civil Servants of the Revolutionary Period." *Pa Mag Hist*, LXXV (1951), 159-169.

4 COMETTI, Elizabeth. "Impressment During the American Revolution." In *Walter Clinton Jackson Essays in the Social Sciences*, ed. Vera Largent. Chapel Hill, 1942.

5 FERGUSON, E. James. *The Power of the Purse: A History of American Public Finance, 1776-1790*. Chapel Hill, 1961.†

6 GAINES, William H. J. "The Forgotten Army: Recruiting for a National Emergency." *Va Mag Hist*, LVI (1948), 267-279.

7 HANDLIN, Oscar and Mary. "Revolutionary Economic Policy in Massachusetts." *Wm Mar Q*, 3d ser., IV (1947), 3-26.

8 HARLOW, Ralph V. "Aspects of Revolutionary Finance, 1775-1783." *Am Hist Rev*, XXXV (1929), 46-68.

9 HASKETT, Richard C. "Prosecuting the Revolution." *Am Hist Rev*, LIX (1954), 578-587.

10 HUNT, Agnes. *The Provincial Committees of Safety of the American Revolution*. Cleveland, 1904.

11 JAMESON, Hugh. "Equipment for the Militia of the Middle States, 1775-1781." *J Am Mil Inst*, III (1939), 26-38.

12 JAMESON, Hugh. "Subsistence for Middle States Militia, 1776-1781." *Mil Affairs*, XXX (1966), 121-134.

13 LEONARD, Eugenie A. "Paper as a Critical Commodity During the American Revolution." *Pa Mag Hist*, LXXIV (1950), 488-499.

14 MORSE, Sidney G. "State or Continental Privateers?" *Am Hist Rev*, LII (1946), 68-73.

15 MURPHY, Orville T. "The American Revolutionary Army and the Concept of *Levée en Masse*." *Mil Affairs*, XXIII (1959), 13-20.

16 NEUMANN, George C. *The History of Weapons of the American Revolution*. New York, 1967.

17 NORTON, William B. "Paper Currency in Massachusetts During the Revolution." *N Eng Q*, VII (1934), 43-69.

18 PINKETT, Harold T. "Maryland as a Source of Food Supplies During the American Revolution." *Md Hist Mag*, XLVI (1951), 157-172.

19 REYNOLDS, Donald E. "Ammunition Supply in Revolutionary Virginia." *Va Mag Hist*, LXXIII (1965), 56-77.

20 SCOTT, Kenneth. "Price Control in New England During the Revolution." *N Eng Q*, XIX (1946), 453-473.

21 SMITH, Jonathan. "How Massachusetts Raised Her Troops in the Revolution." *Proc Mass Hist Soc*, LV (1923), 345-370.

1 STEPHENSON, Orlando W. "The Supply of Gunpowder in 1776." *Am Hist Rev*, XXX (1925), 271-281.

2 VER STEEG, Clarence L. "Stacey Hepburn and Company: Enterprisers in the American Revolution." *S C Hist Mag*, LV (1954), 1-5.

3 WHEELER, E. Milton. "Development and Organization of the North Carolina Militia." *N C Hist Rev*, LXI (1964), 307-323.

4 WHITAKER, Bessie L. *The Provincial Council and Committees of Safety in North Carolina*. Chapel Hill, 1908.

5 YOUNG, Henry J. "Treason and Its Punishment in Revolutionary Pennsylvania." *Pa Mag Hist*, XC (1966), 287-313.

2. Warfare and External Relations

A. THE INTERNATIONAL SETTING

6 Library of Congress. *List of Works Relating to the French Alliance in the American Revolution*. Washington, D.C., 1907.

7 ALDEN, Dauril. "The Marquis of Pombal and the American Revolution." *Americas*, XVII (1961), 369-382.

8 AUGUR, Helen. *The Secret War of Independence*. New York and Boston, 1955.

9 AUPHAN, P. "Les Communications entre la France et l'Amérique pendant la Guerre de l'Indépendence Américaine." *Revue Maritime*, n.s., Nos. 63-64 (1925), 331-348, 497-517.

10 BARTON, H. Arnold. "Sweden and the War of American Independence." *Wm Mar Q*, 3d ser., XXIII (1966), 408-430.

11 BEIRNE, Francis F. "Mission to Canada, 1776." *Md Hist Mag*, LX (1965), 404-420.

12 BEMIS, Samuel F. *The Diplomacy of the American Revolution*. New York, 1935; Bloomington, 1957.†

13 BEMIS, Samuel F. *The Hussey-Cumberland Mission and American Independence*. Princeton, 1931.

14 BENSON, Adolph B. *Sweden and the American Revolution*. New Haven, 1926.

15 BROWN, Margaret L. "William Bingham, Agent of the Continental Congress in Martinique." *Pa Mag Hist*, LXI (1937), 54-87.

16 BROWN, Vera L. *Anglo-Spanish Relations in America in the Closing Years of the Colonial Era (1763-1774)*. Baltimore, 1923.

17 CONROTTE, Manuel. *La intervención de España en la independencia de los Estados Unidos de la Am´erica del Norte*. Madrid, 1920.

18 CORWIN, Edward S. *French Policy and the American Alliance of 1778*. Princeton, 1916.

1 DONIOL, Henri. *Histoire de la Participation de la France à l'Etablissement des Etats-Unis d'Amérique; Correspondence et Documents.* 5 vols. Paris, 1886-1892.

2 DOUGLASS, Elisha P. "German Intellectuals and the American Revolution." *Wm Mar Q*, 3d ser., XVII (1960), 200-218.

3 ECHEVERRIA, Durand. *Mirage in the West: A History of the French Image of American Society to 1815.* Princeton, 1957.†

4 EDLER, Friedrich. *The Dutch Republic and the American Revolution.* Baltimore, 1911.

5 GOLDER, Frank A. "Catherine II and the American Revolution." *Am Hist Rev*, XXI (1915), 92-96.

6 GRAEWE, Richard. "The American Revolution Comes to Hannover." *Wm Mar Q*, 3d ser., XX (1963), 246-250.

7 GRIFFITHS, David M. "American Commercial Diplomacy in Russia, 1780 to 1783." *Wm Mar Q*, 3d ser., XXVII (1970), 379-410.

8 GRIFFITHS, David M. "Nikita Panin, Russian Diplomacy, and the American Revolution." *Slav Rev*, XXXVIII (1969), 1-24.

9 HAIMAN, M. *Poland and the American Revolutionary War.* Washington, D.C., 1932.

10 HORN, D. B. *The British Diplomatic Service, 1689-1789.* Oxford, 1961.

11 HUNNINGHER, Benjamin. "Dutch-American Relations During the Revolution." *N-Y Hist Soc Q*, XXXVII (1953), 170-184.

12 IRVINE, Dallas D. "The Newfoundland Fishery: A French Objective in the War of American Independence." *Canad Hist Rev*, XIII (1932), 268-284.

13 KETCHAM, Ralph L. "France and American Politics, 1763-1793." *Pol Sci Q*, LXXVIII (1963), 198-223.

14 KROGER, Alfred. *Geburt der USA: German Newspaper Accounts of the American Revolution, 1763-1783.* Madison, 1962.

15 MADARIAGA, Isabel de. *Britain, Russia and the Armed Neutrality of 1780.* New Haven, 1962.

16 MALCOLM-SMITH, Elizabeth F. *British Diplomacy in the Eighteenth Century, 1700-1789.* London, 1937.

17 MARTIN, Gaston. "Commercial Relations Between Nantes and the American Colonies During the War of Independence." *J Econ Bus Hist* IV (1932), 812-829.

18 MENG, John J. *The Comte de Vergennes; European Phases of His American Diplomacy (1774-1780).* Washington, D.C., 1932.

19 MORALES PADRON, Francisco. *Spanish Help in American Independence.* Madrid, 1952.

20 MURPHY, Orville T. "Charles Gravier de Vergennes: Portrait of an Old Regime Diplomat." *Pol Sci Q*, LXXXIII (1968), 400-418.

1 PERKINS, James B. *France in the American Revolution.* Boston and New York, 1911.

2 RAMSEY, John F. *Anglo-French Relations, 1763-1770; A Study of Choiseul's Foreign Policy.* Berkeley, 1939.

3 RENAUT, F. P. *Les Provinces-Unies et la Guerre d'Amérique, 1775-1784.* 3 vols. Paris, 1924-1932.

4 STINCHCOMBE, William C. *The American Revolution and the French Alliance.* Syracuse, 1969.

5 STREETER, Floyd B. "The Diplomatic Career of William Carmichael." *Md Hist Mag,* VIII (1913), 119-146.

6 TRUDEL, Marcel. *Louis XVI, le Congrès Américain et le Canada, 1774-1789.* Quebec, 1949.

7 VAN ALSTYNE, Richard W. *Empire and Independence: The International History of the American Revolution.* New York, 1965.†

8 VAN ALSTYNE, Richard W. "Great Britain, the War for Independence, and the 'Gathering Storm' in Europe, 1775-1778." *Hunt Lib Q,* XXVII (1964), 311-346.

9 VAN WINTER, P. J. *Het aandel van der Amsterdamschen handel aan den opbouw van het Amerikaansche gemeenebest.* 2 vols. The Hague, 1927-1933.

10 VARG, Paul. *Foreign Policies of the Founding Fathers.* East Lansing, Mich., 1963.†

11 WHARTON, Francis, ed. *Revolutionary Diplomatic Correspondence.* 6 vols. Washington, D.C., 1889.

12 WIJK, F. W. van. *De republiek en Amerika, 1776-1782.* Leyden, 1921.

B. BRITISH FORCES, STRATEGY, AND POLITICS

13 MANWARING, G. E. *A Bibliography of British Naval History.* London, 1929.

14 ANDERSON, Olive G. "Establishment of British Supremacy at Sea and the Exchange of Prisoners of War, 1689-1783." *Eng Hist Rev,* LXXV (1960), 77-89.

15 ATKINSON, C. T. "British Forces in North America, 1774-1781: Their Distribution and Strength." *J Soc Army Hist Res,* XVI (1937), 3-23.

16 BILLIAS, George A., ed. *George Washington's Opponents.* New York, 1969.†

17 BINNEY, J. E. D. *British Public Finance and Administration, 1774-92.* Oxford and New York, 1958.

18 BRADFORD, S. Sydney. "The Common British Soldier—From the Journal of Thomas Sullivan, 49th Regiment of Foot." *Md Hist Mag,* LXII (1967), 219-253.

1   BURNS, R. E. "Ireland and British Military Preparations for War in America in 1775." *Cithara*, II (1963), 42-61.

2   CLINTON, Henry. *The American Rebellion: Sir Henry Clinton's Narrative of His Campaigns, 1775-1782*. . . . Ed. William B. Willcox. New Haven, 1954.

3   COLEMAN, John M. "Joseph Galloway and the British Occupation of Philadelphia." *Pa Hist*, XXX (1963), 272-300.

4   CRISPIN, B. "Clyde Shipping and the American War." *Scot Hist Rev*, XLI (1962), 124-134.

5   CRUIKSHANK, E. A. "The King's Royal Regiment of New York." *Pap Ontario Hist Soc*, XXVII (1931), 193-324.

6   CUNEO, John R. "The Early Days of the Queen's Rangers, August 1776—February 1777." *Mil Affairs*, XXII (1958), 65-74.

7   CURTIS, Edward E. *Organization of the British Army in the American Revolution*. London and New Haven, 1926.

8   DABNEY, William M. *After Saratoga: The Story of the Convention Army*. Albuquerque, 1954.

9   EELKING, Max von. *German Allied Troops in the North American War*. Albany, 1893.

10 FAGERSTROM, Dalphy I. "Scottish Opinion and the American Revolution." *Wm Mar Q*, 3d ser., XI (1954), 252-275.

11 FORD, Worthington C. "Parliament and the Howes." *Proc Mass Hist Soc*, XLIV (1910), 120-175.

12 FORTESCUE, John W. *A History of the British Army*. 13 vols. and 6 atlases. London and New York, 1899-1920.

13 FULLER, J. F. C. "The Revival and Training of Light Infantry in the British Army, 1757-1806." *J Roy Un Serv Inst*, LVII (1913), 1187-1214.

14 GRUBER, Ira D. "Lord Howe and the Lord George Germain: British Politics and the Winning of American Independence." *Wm Mar Q*, 3d ser., XXII (1965), 225-243.

15 HAYES, James. "The Royal House of Hanover and the British Army, 1714-1760." *Bull J Ry Lib*, XL (1957-1958), 328-357.

16 JAMES, William M. *The British Navy in Adversity: A Study of the War of American Independence*. London, 1926.

17 LINGLEY, Charles R. "The Treatment of Burgoyne's Troops Under the Saratoga Convention." *Pol Sci Q*, XXII (1907), 440-459.

18 LOWELL, E. J. *The Hessians and Other German Auxiliaries of Great Britain in the Revolutionary War*. New York, 1884; repr. 1965.

19 LUTNICK, Solomon. *The American Revolution and the British Press, 1775-1783*. Columbia, S.C., 1967.

20 MACKESY, Piers. "British Strategy in the War of American Independence." *Yale Review*, LII (1963), 539-557.

1 MACKESY, Piers. *The War for America, 1775-1783.* Cambridge, Mass., 1964.

2 MARCUS, Geoffrey J. *The Formative Centuries.* Vol. I of *A Naval History of England.* London, 1961.

3 RIEDESEL, Baroness von. *Baroness von Riedesel and the American Revolution: Journal and Correspondence of a Tour of Duty, 1776-1783.* Trans. Marvin L. Brown, Jr. Chapel Hill, 1965.

4 SCHUYLER, Robert L. "The Rise of Anti-Imperialsim in England." *Pol Sci Q,* XXVII (1922), 440-471.

5 SMITH, Paul H. *Loyalists and Redcoats: A Study in British Revolutionary Policy.* Chapel Hill, 1964.†

6 SOSIN, Jack M. "The Use of Indians in the War of the American Revolution: A Re-Assessment of Responsibility." *Canad Hist Rev,* XLVI (1965), 101-121.

7 SPARROW, W. J. "Benjamin Thompson and Lord George Germain." *U Birmingham Hist J,* V (1956), 138-146.

8 STADTLER, Erich. *Die Ansback-Bayreuther Truppen im Amerikanischen Unabhängigkeitskrieg, 1777-1783.* Nürnberg, 1956.

9 SYRETT, David *Shipping and the American War 1775-83: A Study of British Transport Organization.* London, 1970.

10 SYRETT, David. "The West India Merchants and the Conveyance of the King's Troops to the Caribbean, 1779-1782." *J Soc Army Hist Res,* XL (1967), 169-176.

11 TATUM, Edward H., ed. *The American Journal of Ambrose Serle, Secretary to Lord Howe, 1776-1778.* San Marino, Calif., 1940.

12 TEMPERLEY, Harold. "Chatham, North, and America." *Q Rev,* CCXXI (1914), 295-319.

13 TOWER, Charlemagne. *Essays Political and Historical.* Philadelphia and London, 1914.

14 UHLENDORF, Bernard A., ed. *Revolution in America: Confidential Letters and Journals, 1776-1784 of Adjutant General Major Baurmeister of the Hessian Forces.* New Brunswick, 1957.

15 USHER, Roland G., Jr. "Royal Navy Impressment During the American Revolution." *Miss Val Hist Rev,* XXXVII (1951), 673-688.

16 WESTERN, John R. *The English Militia in the Eighteenth Century: The Story of a Political Issue, 1660-1802.* London and Toronto, 1965.

17 WHITE, Herbert H. "British Prisoners of War in Hartford During the Revolution." *Bull Conn Hist Soc,* XIX (1954), 65-81.

18 WILLCOX, William B. "British Strategy in America, 1778." *J Mod Hist,* XIX (1947), 97-121.

19 WILLCOX, William B. "Rhode Island in British Strategy, 1780-1781." *J Mod Hist,* XVII (1945), 304-331.

1 WILLCOX, William B. "Why Did the British Lose the American Revolution?" *Mich Alum Q Rev*, LXII (1956), 317-324.

2 WILLIAMS, Basil. "Charles Fox and the Amerian Revolution." *Q Rev*, CCXXKV (1915), 426-443. (A review essay.)

C. AMERICAN FORCES AND STRATEGY

3 ABELL, Francis. *Prisoners of War in Britain 1756 to 1815; A Record of Their Lives, Their Romance and Their Sufferings.* London and New York, 1914.

4 ADAMS, Charles F. *Studies Military and Diplomatic, 1775-1865.* New York, 1911.

5 ALEXANDER, Arthur J. "Desertion and Its Punishment in Revolutionary Virginia." *Wm Mar Q*, 3d ser., III (1946), 383-397.

6 ALEXANDER, Arthur J. "A Footnote on Deserters from the Virginia Forces During the American Revolution." *Va Mag Hist*, LV (1947), 137-146.

7 ALLEN, Gardner W. *Massachusetts Privateers of the Revolution Coll Mass Hist Soc*, LXXVII (1927).

8 ALLEN, Gardner W. *A Naval History of the American Revolution.* 2 vols. Boston, 1913.

9 ANDERSON, Olive. "The Treatment of Prisoners of War in Britain During the American War of Independence." *Bull Inst Hist Res*, XXVIII (1955), 63-83.

10 APPLEGATE, Howard L. "The Medical Administrators of the American Revolutionary Army." *Mil Affairs*, XXV (1961), 1-10.

11 BALCH, Thomas. *The French in America During the War of Independence.* 2 vols. Philadelphia, 1891-1895.

12 BATCHELLOR, Albert S. "The Ranger Service in the Upper Valley of the Connecticut, and the Most Northerly Regiment of New Hampshire Militia in the Period of the Revolution." *Mag Hist*, VI (1907), 187-205, 249-268.

13 BERNATH, Stuart L. "George Washington and the Genesis of American Military Discipline." *Mid-America*, XLIX (1967), 83-100.

14 BILLIAS, George A., ed. *George Washington's Generals.* New York, 1964.†

15 BOLTON, Charles K. *The Private Soldier Under Washington.* New York, 1902.

16 BOUVET, Maurice. *Le Service de Santé Français pendant la Guerre d'Indépendance des Etats-Unis.* Paris, 1934.

17 BOWMAN, Allen. *The Morale of the American Revolutionary Army.* Washington, D.C., 1943.

18 CARSON, Hampton L. "Washington at Valley Forge." *Pa Mag Hist*, XLIII (1919), 97-116.

1 CLARK, William B. *Ben Franklin's Privateers: A Naval Epic of the American Revolution.* Baton Rouge, 1956.

2 CLARK, William B. *George Washington's Navy: Being an Account of His Excellency's Fleet in New England Waters.* Baton Rouge, 1960.

3 CLOSEN, Baron Ludwig von. *The Revolutionary Journal of Baron Ludwig von Closen, 1780-1783.* Trans. and ed. Evelyn M. Acomb. Chapel Hill, 1958.

4 COGGINS, Jack. *Ships and Seamen of the American Revolution: Vessels, Crews, Weapons, Gear, Naval Tactics, and Actions of the War for Independence.* Harrisburg, Pa., 1969.

5 DANDRIDGE, D. *American Prisoners of the Revolution.* Charlottesville, Va., 1911.

6 ECHEVARRIA, Durand, and Orville T. MURPHY. "The American Revolutionary Army: A French Estimate in 1777." *Mil Affairs*, XXVII (1963), 1-7, 153-162.

7 EDWARDS, William W. "Morgan and His Riflemen." *Wm Mar Q*, XXIII (1914), 73-106.

8 FORBES, Allen. "Marches and Camp Sites of the French Army in New England During the Revolutionary War." *Proc Mass Hist Soc*, LVIII (1925), 267-285.

9 GIBSON, J. E. *Dr Bodo Otto and the Medical Background of the American Revolution.* Springfield, Mass., 1937.

10 GOTTSCHALK, Louis. "The Attitude of European Officers in the Revolutionary Armies Toward General George Washington." *J Ill St Hist Soc*, XXXII (1939), 20-50.

11 GREENE, Francis V. *The Revolutionary War and the Military Policy of the United States.* New York, 1911.

12 GREENWOOD, Isaac J. *Captain John Manley, Second in Rank in the United States Navy, 1776-1783.* Boston, 1915.

13 HATCH, Louis C. *The Administration of the American Revolutionary Army.* New York, 1904.

14 HOWE, Octavious T. "Beverly Privateers in the American Revolution." *Pub Col Soc Mass*, XXIV (1934), 318-435.

15 JOHNSON, Victor L. *The Administration of the American Commissariat During the Revolutionary War.* Philadelphia, 1941.

16 MAURER, Maurer. "Military Justice Under General Washington." *Mil Affairs*, XXVIII (1964), 8-16.

17 MERLANT, Joachim. *Soldiers and Sailors of France in the American War of Independence.* New York, 1920.

18 MONTROSS, Lynn. *Rag, Tag and Bobtail: The Story of the Continental Army, 1775-1783.* New York, 1952.

19 NASH, Frank. "The Continental Line of North Carolina." *N C Booklet*, XVII (1918), 105-134.

1 PAULLIN, Charles O. "The Connecticut Navy of the American Revolution." *N Eng Mag*, XXXV (1907), 714-725.

2 PAULLIN, Charles O. "The Massachusetts Navy of the American Revolution." *N Eng Mag*, XXXV (1907), 571-578.

3 PAULLIN, Charles O. *The Navy of the American Revolution; Its Administration, Its Policy, and Its Achievements.* Cleveland, 1906.

4 RANKIN, Hugh F. *The North Carolina Continentals.* Chapel Hill, 1971.

5 REICHMAN, Felix. "The Pennsylvania Rifle: A Social Interpretation of Changing Military Techniques." *Pa Mag Hist*, LXIX (1945), 3-14.

6 SLOANE, William M. "Von Moltke's View of Washington's Strategy." *Century*, LXXIII (1907), 517-524.

7 SPENCER, Richard H. "Pulaksi's Legion." *Md Hist Mag*, XIII (1918), 214-226.

8 STUTESMAN, John H., Jr. "Colonel Armand and Washington's Cavalry." *N-Y Hist Soc Q*, XLV (1961), 5-42.

9 TYLER, Lyon G. "The Old Virginia Line in the Middle States During the American Revolution." *Tyler's Q Hist Gen Mag*, XII (1930), 1-42. 90-141.

10 VAN DOREN, Carl. *Mutiny in January.* New York, 1943.

11 VERMEULE, Cornelius C. "Number of Soldiers in the Revolution." *Proc N J Hist Soc*, n.s., VII (1922), 223-227.

12 VERMEULE, Cornelius C. "Service of the New Jersey Militia in the Revolutionary War." *Proc N J Hist Soc*, n.s., IX (1924), 234-248.

13 WARD, Christopher. *The Delaware Continentals, 1776-1783.* Wilmington, 1941.

14 WRIGHT, John W. "Notes on the Continental Army." *Wm Mar Q*, 2d ser., XI (1931), 81-105, 185-209; XII (1932), 79-104; XIII (1933), 85-97.

15 WRIGHT, John W. "The Rifle in the American Revolution." *Am Hist Rev*, XXIX (1924), 293-299.

D. MILITARY OPERATIONS
(General works are followed by special studies, beginning with 90.8, arranged chronologically.)

16 HIGGINBOTHAM, Don. "American Historians and the Military History of the American Revolution." *Am Hist Rev*, LXX (1964), 18-34.

17 ADAMS, Charles Francis. *Studies Military and Diplomatic, 1775-1865.* New York, 1911.

18 CARRINGTON, Henry B. *Battles of the American Revolution, 1775-1781.* New York, 1876.

19 CLARK, William B., ed. *Naval Documents of the American Revolution . . . .* 4 vols., in progress. Washington, D.C., 1964- .

20 LOSSING, Benson J. *The Pictorial Field Book of the Revolution.* 2 vols. New York, 1851-1852.

1 MAHAM, Alfred T. *The Major Operations of the Navies in the American War of Independence.* Boston, 1913.

2 MIDDLEBROOK, Louis F. *Maritime Connecticut During the American Revolution.* 2 vols. Salem, Mass., 1925.

3 PECKHAM, Howard H. *The War for Independence: A Military History.* Chicago, 1958.

4 SCHEER, George F., and Hugh J. RANKIN, eds. *Rebels and Redcoats,* Cleveland, 1957.

5 WALLACE, Willard M. *Appeal to Arms: A Military History of the American Revolution.* New York, 1951.†

6 WARD, Christopher. *The War of the Revolution.* Ed. John R. Alden. 2 vols. New York, 1952.

7 WELLER, Jac. "Irregular but Effective: Partisan Weapons and Tactics in the American Revolution, Southern Theatre." *Mil Affairs,* XXI (1957), 119-131.

8 TOURTELLOT, Arthur B. *A Bibliogrpahy of the Battles of Lexington and Concord.* New York, 1959.

9 ALDEN, John R. "Why the March to Concord?" *Am Hist Rev,* XLIX (1944), 446-454.

10 FRENCH, Allen. *General Gage's Informers.* Ann Arbor, 1932.

11 FRENCH, Allen. *Day of Lexington and Concord.* Boston, 1925.

12 FRENCH, Allen. *The First Year of the American Revolution.* Boston and New York, 1934.

13 FROTHINGHAM, Richard. *History of the Siege of Boston, and of the Battles of Lexington, Concord and Bunker Hill.* 4th ed. Boston, 1873.

14 MURDOCK, Harold. *The Nineteenth of April, 1775.* Boston, 1923.

15 TOURTELLOT, Arthur B. *William Diamond's Drum.* New York, 1959.

16 FLEMING, Thomas. *Now We Are Enemies.* New York, 1960. (On Bunker Hill.)

17 COHEN, Joel A. "Lexington and Concord: Rhode Island Reacts." *R I Hist,* XXVI (1967), 97-102.

18 KETCHUM, Richard. *The Battle for Bunker Hill.* New York, 1962.

19 KNOLLENBERG, Bernhard. "Bunker Hill Re-viewed: A Study of the Conflict of Historical Evidence." *Proc Mass Hist Soc,* LXXII (1957-1960), 84-100.

20 MURDOCK, Harold. *Bunker Hill, Notes and Queries on a Famous Battle.* Boston, 1927.

21 ROBERTS, Kenneth L. *March to Quebec.* 4th ed. Garden City, N.Y., 1942.

22 MEREDITH, R. Brian. "Carleton, Montgomery, Arnold." *Dalhousie Rev,* VII (1928), 390-400.

1   NAISAWALD, Louis van L. "Robert Howe's Operations in Virginia, 1775-1776." *Va Mag Hist*, LX (1952), 437-443.

2   MOOMAW, William H. "The British Leave Colonial Virginia." *Va Mag Hist*, LXVI (1958), 147-160.

3   HARASZTI, Zoltan. "Besieging Boston with a Dwindling Army; The Last Stages of the Siege of Boston." *More Books*, VII (1932), 123-138, 219-228.

4   BUTTERFIELD, Lyman H. "Psychological Warfare in 1776: The Jefferson-Franklin Plan to Cause Hessian Desertions." *Proc Am Philos Soc*, XCIV (1950), 233-241.   5

5   GERLACH, Don R. "Philip Schuyler and 'The Road to Glory': A Question of Loyalty and Competence." *N-Y Hist Soc Q*, XLIV (1965), 341-386.

6   RANKIN, Hugh F. "The Moore's Creek Bridge Campaign, 1776." *N C Hist Rev*, XXX (1953), 23-60.

7   ADAMS, Randolph G. "Cartography of the British Attack on Fort Moultrie in 1776." In *Essays Offered to Herbert Putnam*, ed. W. W. Bishop and A. Keough. New Haven, 1929.

8   ROBSON, Eric. "The Expedition to the Southern Colonies, 1775-1776." *Eng Hist Rev*, LXVI (1951), 535-560.

9   GANYARD, Robert L. "Threat from the West: North Carolina and the Cherokee, 1776-1778." *N C Hist Rev*, XLV (1968), 47-66.

10   BLIVEN, Bruce. *Battle for Manhattan*. New York, 1956.†

11   JOHNSTON, Henry P. *Campaign of 1776 Around New York and Brooklyn*. Brooklyn, 1876.

12   KOKE, Richard J. "The Struggle for the Hudson: The British Naval Expedition Under Captain Hyde Parker and Captian James Wallace, July 12-August 18, 1776." *N-Y Hist Soc Q*, XL (1956), 114-175.

13   PALTSITS, Victor H. "The Jeopardy of Washington, September 15, 1776." *N-Y Hist Soc Q*, XXXII (1948), 253-268.

14   JOHNSTON, Henry P. *Battle of Harlem Heights, September 16, 1776*. New York, 1897.

15   BILLIAS, George A. "Pelham Bay: A Forgotten Battle." *N-Y Hist Soc Q*, XLII (1958), 20-38.

16   BILL, Alfred H. *The Campaign of Princeton, 1776-1777*. Princeton, 1948.

17   SMITH, Samuel S. *The Battle of Princeton*. Monmouth Beach, N.J., 1967.

18   SMITH, Samuel S. *The Battle of Trenton*. Monmouth Beach, N.J., 1965.

19   STRYKER, W. S. *Battles of Trenton and Princeton*. Boston, 1898.

20   CADWALADER, John. "Prelude to Valley Forge." *Pa Mag Hist*, LXXXII (1958), 466-471.

1 BIRD, Harrison. *March to Saratoga: General Burgoyne and the American Campaign, 1777.* New York, 1963.

2 CLARK, Jane. "The Command of the Canadian Army for the Campaign of 1777." *Canad Hist Rev*, X (1929), 129-135.

3 CLARK, Jane. "Responsibility for the Failure of the Burgoyne Campaign." *Am Hist Rev*, XXXV (1930), 542-559.

4 NICKERSON, Hoffman. *The Turning Point of the Revolution.* Boston, 1928.

5 HALL, Hiland. *Battle of Bennington.* Milford, Mass., 1877.

6 LANSING, Amy E. "Baum's Raid." *N Y St Hist Assn Q J*, IX (1928), 45-56.

7 LUTWICK, Solomon. "The American Victory at Saratoga: A View from the British Press." *N Y Hist*, XLIV (1963), 103-128.

8 MOOMAW, William H. "The Denouement of General Howe's Campaign of 1777." *Eng Hist Rev*, LXXIX (1964), 498-512.

9 SHIPTON, Nathaniel N. "General Joseph Palmer: Scapegoat for the Rhode Island Fiasco of October, 1777." *N Eng Q*, XXXIX (1966), 498-512.

10 BAURMEISTER, C. L. *Letters from Major Baurmeister to Colonel von Jungkenn Written During the Philadelphia Campaign, 1777-1778.* Philadelphia, 1937.

11 BILL, Alfred H. *Valley Forge: The Making of an Army.* New York, 1952.

12 BROWN, Gerald S. "The Anglo-French Naval Crisis, 1778: A Study of Conflict in the North Cabinet." *Wm Mar Q*, 3d ser., XIII (1956), 3-25.

13 "Proceedings of a General Court Martial . . . ." *Coll N-Y Hist Soc*, 1873 (New York, 1874), pp. 1-208. (On the Battle of Monmouth, 1778.)

14 SMITH, Samuel S. *The Battle of Monmouth.* Monmouth Beach, N.J., 1964.

15 STRYKER, William S. *The Battle of Monmouth.* Princeton, 1927.

16 ABBEY, Kathryn T. "Peter Chester's Defense of the Mississippi After the Willing Raid." *Miss Val Hist Rev*, XXII (1935), 17-32.

17 BULLEN, Ripley P. "Fort Tonyn and the Campaign of 1778." *Fla Hist Q*, XXIX (1951), 253-260.

18 CAUGHEY, John. "Willing's Expedition down the Mississippi, 1778." *La Hist Q*, XV (1932), 5-36.

19 OLSON, Gary D. "Thomas Brown, Loyalist Partisan, and the Revolutionary War in Georgia, 1777-1782." *Ga Hist Q*, LIV (1970), 1-19, 183-208.

20 LAWRENCE, Alexander A. "General Robert Howe and the British Capture of Savannah in 1778." *Ga Hist Q*, XXXVI (1952), 303-327.

21 LAWRENCE, Alexander A. *Storm over Savannah: The Story of Count d'Estaing and the Siege of the Town in 1779.* Athens, Ga., 1951.

1 MURPHY, W. S. "The Irish Brigade of France at the Siege of Savannah, 1779." *Ga Hist Q*, XXXVIII (1954), 307-321.

2 ASHMORE, Otis, and C. H. OLMSTEAD. "The Battles of Kettle Creek and Brier Creek." *Ga Hist Q*, X (1926), 85-125.

3 JOHNSTON, Henry P. *Storming of Stony Point.* New York, 1900.

4 New York, Division of Archives and History. *The Sullivan-Clinton Campaign in 1779. Chronology and Selected Documents.* Albany, 1929.

5 NORTON, A. T. *History of Sullivan's Campaign Against the Iroquois.* Lima, N.Y., 1879.

6 PARKER, Arthur C. "The Indian Interpretation of the Sullivan-Clinton Campaign." *Pub Roch Hist Soc*, VIII (1929), 45-59.

7 BARNHART, John D. "A New Evaluation of Henry Hamilton and George Rogers Clark." *Miss Val Hist Rev*, XXXVII (1951), 643-652.

8 LEE, Henry (1756-1818). *Memoirs of the War in the Southern Department of the United States.* 2nd ed. Washington, D.C., 1827.

9 PUGH, Robert C. "The Revolutionary Militia in the Southern Campaign, 1780-1781." *Wm Mar Q*, 3d ser., XIV (1957), 154-175.

10 TARLETON, Banastre. *History of the Campaigns, 1780-1781.* London, 1787.

11 WEIGLEY, Russell F. *The Partisan War: The South Carolina Campaign of 1780-1782.* Columbia, S.C., 1970.†

12 UHLENDORF, Bernard A., ed. *The Siege of Charleston.* Ann Arbor, 1938.

13 DRAPER, Lyman C. *King's Mountain and Its Heroes.* Cincinnati, 1881.

14 DAVIS, Burke. *The Cowpens-Guilford Campaign.* Philadelphia, 1962.

15 RANKIN, Hugh F. "Cowpens: Prelude to Yorktown." *N C Hist Rev*, XXXI (1954), 336-369.

16 TREACY, M. F. *Prelude to Yorktown: The Southern Campaign of Nathanael Greene, 1780-1781.* Chapel Hill, 1963.

17 JOHNSTON, Henry P. *The Yorktown Campaign and the Surrender of Cornwallis, 1781.* New York, 1881.

18 KYTE, George W. "Strategic Blunder: Lord Cornwallis Abandons the Carolinas." *Historian*, XXII (1960), 129-144.

19 KYTE, George W. "General Wayne Marches South, 1781." *Pa Hist*, XXX (1963), 301-315.

20 LEE, Henry (1787-1837). *Campaign of 1781 in the Carolinas.* Philadelphia, 1824; repr. Chicago, 1962.

21 WILLCOX, William B. "The British Road to Yorktown: A Study in Divided Command." *Am Hist Rev*, LII (1946), 1-35.

1 FLEMING, Thomas J. *Beat the Last Drum*. New York, 1963.

2 LARRABEE, Harold A. *Decision at the Chesapeake*. New York, 1964.

3 ADAMS, Randolph G. "A View of Cornwallis's Surrender at Yorktown." *Am Hist Rev*, XXXVII (1931), 25-49.

4 LUTNICK, Solomon M. "The Defeat at Yorktown: A View from the British Press." *Va Mag Hist*, LXXII (1964), 471-478.

5 WRIGHT, John W. "Notes on the Siege of Yorktown in 1781 with Special Reference to the Conduct of a Siege in the Eighteenth Century." *Wm Mar Q*, 2d ser., XII (1932), 229-249.

6 JOHNSTON, James A. "The War Did Not End at Yorktown." *Va Mag Hist*, LX (1952), 444-457.

7 KINNAIRD, Lawrence. "The Spanish Expedition Against Fort St. Joseph in 1781; A New Interpretation." *Miss Val Hist Rev*, XIX (1932), 173-191.

8 KYTE, George W. "A Projected British Attack upon Philadelphia in 1781." *Pa Mag Hist*, LXXVI (1952), 379-393.

9 KYTE, George W. "General Greene's Plans for the Capture of Charleston, 1781-1782." *S C Hist Mag*, LXI (1961), 96-106.

10 HUMPHREYS, R. A. "Richard Oswald's Plan for an English and Russian Attack on Spanish America, 1781-1782." *His-Am Hist Rev*, XVIII (1938), 95-101.

11 BARNWELL, Joseph W. "The Evacuation of Charleston by the British in 1782." *S C Hist Mag*, XI (1910), 1-26.

12 HOLMES, Jack D. L. "Robert Ross's Plan for an English Invasion of Louisiana in 1782." *La Hist Q*, V (1964), 161-177.

E. THE NEGOTIATION OF PEACE

13 BERNARDY, Amy A. "La Mission di Beniamino Franklin a Parigi nei dispacci degli ambasciatori Veneziani in Francia (1776-1786)." *ASI*, LXXVIII (1920), 237-262.

14 BROWN, Marvin L., Jr., trans. and ed. *American Independence Through Prussian Eyes: A Neutral View of the Peace Negotiations of 1782-1783. Selections from the Prussian Diplomatic Correspondence*. Durham, N.C., 1959.

15 CHRISTIE, Ian R. *The End of North's Ministry, 1780-1782*. London, 1958.

16 MORRIS, Richard B. *The Peacemakers: The Great Powers and American Independence*. New York, 1965.†

17 MURPHY, Orville T. "The Comte de Vergennes, the Newfoundland Fisheries, and the Peace Negotiations of 1783: A Reconsideration." *Canad Hist Rev*, XLVI (1965), 32-46.

1 SMITH, Paul H. "Sir Guy Carleton, Peace Negotiations, and the Evacuation of New York." *Canad Hist Rev*, L (1969), 245-264.

2 WEAD, Eunice. "British Public Opinion of the Peace with America, 1782." *Am Hist Rev*, XXXIV (1929), 513-531.

3. The Impact of the War on Society

A. THE REVOLUTIONARY MENTALITY
See 4.14, 6.6, 6.20, 35.10.

3 BAILYN, Bernard. *The Ideological Origins of the American Revolution.* Cambridge, Mass., 1956. See also 22.10.

4 BAILYN, Bernard. "Religion and Revolution: Three Biographical Studies." *Perspectives in American History*, IV (1970), 85-169.

5 BERGER, Carl. *Broadsides and Bayonets: The Propaganda War of the American Revolution.* Philadelphia, 1961.

6 BOLLER, Paul F., Jr. "George Washington and Religious Liberty." *Wm Mar Q*, 3d ser., XVII (1960), 486-506.

7 BROWN, Ralph A. "New Hampshire Editors Win the War; A Study in Revolutionary Press Propaganda." *N Eng Q*, XII (1939), 35-51.

8 BUMSTED, John M., and Charles E. CLARK. "New England's Tom Paine: John Allen and the Spirit of Liberty." *Wm Mar Q*, 3d ser., XXI (1964), 561-570.

9 CHAPIN, Bradley. *The American Law of Treason: Revolutionary and Early National Origins.* Seattle, 1964.

10 COMETTI, Elizabeth. "Morals and the American Revolution; Efforts to Curb Luxury, Dissipation, and Extravagance." *S Atl Q*, XLVI (1947), 62-71.

11 DAVIDSON, Philip G. *Propaganda and the American Revolution, 1763-1783.* Chapel Hill, 1941.†

12 DION, Léon. "Natural Law and Manifest Destiny in the Era of the American Revolution." *Canad J Econ Pol Sci*, XXIII (1957), 227-247.

13 DUTCHER, George M. "The Rise of Republican Government in the United States." *Pol Sci Q*, LV (1940), 199-216.

14 ECHEVERRIA, Durand, trans. and ed. "The American Character: A Frenchman Views the New Republic from Philadelphia, 1777." *Wm Mar Q*, 3d ser., XVI (1959), 376-413.

15 FORD, Worthington C. "The Language of War." *Proc Bunker Hill Mon Assn*, (1915), 33-51.

16 GRANGER, Bruce I. *Political Satire in the American Revolution, 1763-1783.* Ithaca, N.Y., 1960.

17 GREEN, Fletcher M. "The Spirit of '76." *Emory Univ Q*, XI (1955), 65-82.

1 HANDLIN, Oscar and Mary, eds. *The Popular Sources of Political Authority: Documents on the Massachusetts Constitution of 1780.* Cambridge, Mass., 1966.

2 HARTZ, Louis. "American Political Thought and the American Revolution." *Am Pol Sci Rev*, XLVI (1952), 321-342.

3 HOLDEN, James A. "Influence of the Death of Jane McCrea on the Burgoyne Campaign." *Proc N Y St Hist Assn*, XII (1913), 249-294.

4 HOOKER, Richard J. "The American Revolution Seen Through a Wine Glass." *Wm Mar Q*, XI (1954), 52-77.

5 KAMMEN, Michael. "The Meaning of Colonization in American Revolutionary Thought." *J Hist Ideas*, XXXI (1970), 337-358.

6 KENYON, Cecelia M. "Alexander Hamilton: Rousseau of the Right." *Pol Sci Q*, LXXIII (1958), 161-178.

7 KENYON, Cecelia M. "Where Paine Went Wrong." *Am Pol Sci Rev*, XLV (1951), 1086-1099.

8 KERR, Harry P. "Politics and Religion in Colonial Fast and Thanksgiving Sermons, 1763-1783." *Q J Sp*, XLVI (1960), 372-382.

9 KETCHAM, Ralph L. "James Madison and the Nature of Man." *J Hist Ideas*, XVI (1958), 62-76.

10 KOCH, Adrienne. *Power, Morals, and the Founding Fathers: Essays in the Interpretation of the American Enlightenment.* Ithaca, N.Y., 1961.†

11 LEMISCH, Jesse. "Listening to the 'Inarticulate': William Widger's Dream and the Loyalties of Amerian Revolutionary Seamen in British Prisons." *J Soc Hist*, III (1969), 1-29.

12 LIVINGSTON, William S. "Emigration as a Theoretical Doctrine During the American Revolution." *J Pol*, XIX (1957), 591-615.

13 LYND, Staughton. *Intellectual Origins of American Radicalism.* New York, 1968.†

14 MOORE, Frank. *Songs and Ballads of the American Revolution.* Philadelphia, 1899; repr. Port Washington, N.Y., 1964.

15 MORAIS, Herbert M. *Deism in Eighteenth-Century America.* New York, 1934. See 111.15.

16 MORGAN, Edmund S. "The American Revolution Considered as an Intellectual Movement." In *Paths of American Thought*, ed. Arthur M. Schlesinger, Jr., and Morton White. Boston, 1963.

17 MORRIS, Richard B. "Legalism Versus Revolutionary Doctrine in New England." *N Eng Q*, IV (1931), 195-215.

18 PATTERSON, Samuel W. *The Spirit of the American Revolution, as Revealed in the Poetry of the Period; A Study of American Patriotic Verse from 1760 to 1783.* Boston, 1915.

19 PILCHER, George W. "The Pamphlet War on the Proposed Virginia Anglican Episcopate, 1767-1775." *Hist Mag P E Ch*, XXX (1961), 266-279.

20 REINHOLD, Meyer. "Opponents of Classical Learning in America During the Revolutionary Period." *Proc Am Philos Soc*, CXII (1968), 221-234.

1   RIEMER, Neal, "The Republicanism of James Madison." *Pol Sci Q*, LXIX (1954), 45-64.

2   SILVER, Rollo G. "Benjamin Edes, Trumpeter of Sedition." *Pap Bibliog Soc Am*, XLVII (1953), 248-268.

3   STOURZH, Gerald. "Reason and Power in Benjamin Franklin's Political Thought." *Am Pol Sci Rev*, LXVII (1953), 1092-1115.

4   TATE, Thad W. "The Social Contract in America, 1774-1787: Revolutionary Theory as a Conservative Instrument." *Wm Mar Q*, 3d ser., XXII (1965), 375-391.

5   TYLER, Moses C. *The Literary History of the American Revolution, 1763-1783*. 2 vols. London and New York, 1897.

6   VOSSLER, Otto. "Die Ursprünge der Amerikanischen Revolution von 1776." *Historische Vierteljahrschrift*, XXVI (1931), 573-588.

7   WISHY, Bernard. "John Locke and the Spirit of '76." *Pol Sci Q*, LXXIII (1958), 413-425.

B. LOYALISTS AND OTHER MINORITIES

On Negroes and Indians, see Section III.3.C., as well as Sections V.5. and VI.4. on Indians. On Loyalists, see 85.3, 85.5, 85.6, 86.5, 86.7, 107.17.

8   ADAIR, Douglass, and John A. SCHUTZ, eds. *Peter Oliver's Origin and Progress of the American Rebellion: A Tory View*. San Marino, Calif., 1961.†

9   ANDREANO, Ralph L., and Herbert D. WERNER. "Charleston Loyalists: A Stastistical Note." *S C Hist Mag*, LX (1959), 164-168.

10 ARCHER, Adair P. "The Quaker's Attitude Towards the Revolution." *Wm Mar Q*, 2d ser., I (1921), 167-182.

11 BECKER, Carl L. "John Jay and Peter Van Schaack." In *Every Man His Own Historian; Essays on History and Politics*. New York, 1935.

12 BELL, Whitfield J., Jr. "Physicians and Politics in the Revolution: The Case of Adam Kuhn." *Trans Stud Phila Col Phy*, XXII (1954), 25-31.

13 BENTON, William Allen. *Whig-Loyalism: An Aspect of Political Ideology in the American Revolutionary Era*. Rutherford, N.J., 1969.

14 BOWLES, Francis T. "The Loyalty of Barnstable in the Revolution." *Pub Col Soc Mass*, XXV (1924), 365-348.

15 BROWN, Alan S., ed. "James Simpson's Reports on the Carolina Loyalists, 1779-1780." *J S Hist*, XXI (1955), 513-519.

16 BROWN, Wallace. *The Good Americans: The Loyalists in the American Revolution*. New York, 1969.

17 BROWN, Wallace. *The King's Friends: The Composition and Motives of the American Loyalist Claimants*. Providence, 1965.

18 BROWN, Wallace. "Negroes and the American Revolution." *Hist Today*, XIV (1964), 556-563.

1 CATHCART, William. *The Baptists and the American Revolution.* Philadelphia, 1876.

2 COHEN, William. "Thomas Jefferson and the Problem of Slavery." *J Am Hist*, LVI (1969), 503-526.

3 CRARY, Catherine S. "The Tory and the Spy: The Double Life of James Rivington." *Wm Mar Q*, 3d ser., XVI (1959), 61-72.

4 D'ELIA, Donald J. "Benjamin Rush and the Negro." *J Hist Ideas*, XXX (1969), 413-422.

5 DE MOND, Robert O. *The Loyalists in North Carolina During the Revolution.* Durham, N.C., 1940.

6 DEXTER, Franklin B. "Notes on Some of the New Haven Loyalists, Including Those Graduated at Yale." *Pap N Haven Col Hist Soc*, IX (1918), 19-45.

7 Downes, Randolph C. "Creek-American Relations, 1782-1790." *Ga Hist Q*, XXI (1937), 152-184.

8 EARDLEY-WILMOT, John. *Historical View of the Commission for Enquiring into the Losses, Services, and Claims, of the American Loyalists.* London, 1815.

9 EGERTON, Hugh E., ed. *The Royal Commission on the Losses and Services of American Loyalists, 1783 to 1785, Being the Notes of Mr. Daniel Parker Coke, M.P., One of the Commissioners During That Period.* Oxford, 1915.

10 ELLEFSON, C. Ashley. "Loyalists and Patriots in Georgia During the American Revolution." *Historian*, XXIV (1962), 347-356.

11 FINGERHUT, Eugene R. "Uses and Abuses of the Loyalists' Claims: A Critique of Quantitative Analysis." *Wm Mar Q*, XXV (1968), 245-258.

12 FLICK, Alexander C. *Loyalism in New York During the American Revolution.* London and New York, 1901.

13 FRECH, Laura P. "The Wilmington Committee of Public Safety and the Loyalist Rising of February, 1776." *N C Hist Rev*, XLI (1964), 21-33.

14 GILBERT, G. A. "The Connecticut Loyalists." *Am Hist Rev*, IV (1899), 273-291.

15 GILPIN, Thomas. *Exile in Virginia: With Observations on the Conduct of the Society of Friends During the Revolutionary War.* Philadelphia, 1848.

16 HAMMOND, Otis G. *Tories of New Hampshire in the War of the Revolution.* Concord, N.H., 1917.

17 HANCOCK, Harold B. *The Delaware Loyalists.* Wilmington, 1940.

18 HANCOCK, Harold B. "The Kent County Loyalists." *Del Hist*, VI (1954), 3-24, 92-139.

19 HANCOCK, Harold B. "The New Castle County Loyalists." *Del Hist*, IV (1951), 315-353.

1 HARRELL, Issac S. *Loyalism in Virginia: Chapters in the Economic History of the Revolution.* Durham, N.C., 1926.

2 HARRELL, Issac S. "North Carolina Loyalists." *N C Hist Rev*, III (1926), 575-590.

3 HELLER, Bernard. "The Role of Jews in the American Revolution." *Mich Alum Q Rev*, LXI (1955), 302-312.

4 HONEYMAN, A. Van Doren. "Concerning the New Jersey Loyalists in the Revolution." *Proc N J Hist Soc*, LI (1933), 117-133.

5 HORSMAN, Reginald. *Expansion and American Indian Policy, 1783-1812.* East Lansing, Mich., 1967.

6 JACKSON, Luther P. "Virginia Negro Soldiers and Seamen in the American Revolution." *J Neg Hist*, XXVII (1942), 247-287.

7 JONES, E. Alfred. *The Loyalists of Massachusetts: Their Memorials, Petitions, and Claims.* Boston and London, 1930.

8 JONES, E. Alfred. *The Loyalists of New Jersey.* Newark, 1927.

9 KEESEY, Ruth M. "Loyalism in Bergen County, New Jersey." *Wm Mar Q*, 3d ser., XVIII (1961), 558-576.

10 KYTE, George W. "Some Plans for a Loyalist Stronghold in the Middle Colonies." *Pa Hist*, XVI (1949), 177-190.

11 LABAREE, Leonard W. "The Nature of American Loyalism." *Proc Am Ant Soc*, n.s., LIV (1944), 15-58.

12 LEVETT, Ella P. "Loyalism in Charleston, 1761-1784." *Proc S C Hist Assn*, VI (1935), 3-17.

13 LOGAN, Gwendolyn E. "The Slave in Connecticut During the American Revolution." *Bull Conn Hist Soc*, XXX (1965), 63-80.

14 LOVEJOY, David S. "Samuel Hopkins: Religion, Slavery, and the Revolution." *N Eng Q*, XL (1967), 227-243.

15 MC KEEL, A.J. "New England Quakers and Military Service in the American Revolution." In *Children of Light*, ed. H. H. Brinton. New York, 1938.

16 MAHON, John K. "Anglo-American Methods of Indian Warfare, 1676-1794." *Miss Val Hist Rev*, XLV (1958), 254-275.

17 MATTHEWS, Albert. "Joyce Junior [Chairman of the Committee for Tarring and Feathering in Boston before and during the Revolutionary War]." *Pub Col Soc Mass*, VIII (1906), 90-104.

18 MATTHEWS, Albert. "Joyce Junior Once More." *Coll Mass Hist Soc*, XI (1910), 280-294.

19 MERRITT, Bruce G. "Loyalism and Social Conflict in Revolutionary Deerfield, Massachusetts." *J Am Hist*, LVII (1970), 277-289.

20 METZGER, Charles H. *Catholics and the American Revolution: A Study in Religious Climate.* Chicago, 1962.

Universitas BIBLIOTHECA Ottaviensis

1 MOHR, Walter H. *Federal Indian Relations, 1774-1788.* London and Philadelphia, 1933.

2 MORISON, Samuel E. "The Property of Harrison Gray, Loyalist." *Pub Col Soc Mass*, XIV (1913), 320-350.

3 MORSE, Jarvis M. "The Wanton Family and Rhode Island Loyalism." *R I Hist Soc Coll*, XXXI (1938), 33-44.

4 NELSON, William H. *The American Tory.* Oxford, 1961.

5 NORTON, Mary Beth, ed. "John Randolph's 'Plan of Accommodations.'" *Wm Mar Q*, 3d ser., XXVIII (1971), 103-120.

6 NOTESTEIN, Wallace. "The Western Indians in the Revolution." *Pub O Arch Hist Soc*, XVI (1907), 269-291.

7 OLSON, Gary D. "Loyalists and the American Revolution: Thomas Brown and the South Carolina Backcountry, 1775-1776." *S C Hist Mag*, LXVIII (1967), 201-219; LXIX (1968), 44-56.

8 PENNINGTON, Edward L. "The Anglican Clergy of Pennsylvania in the American Revolution." *Pa Mag Hist*, LXIII (1939), 401-431.

9 PRESTON, Howard. "Rhode Island and the Loyalists." *R I Hist Soc Coll*, XXI (1928), 109-116; XXII (1929), 5-10.

10 QUARLES, Benjamin. *The Negro in the American Revolution.* Chapel Hill, 1961.†

11 RYERSON, Edgerton. *Loyalists of America and Their Times: From 1620-1816.* 2 vols. Toronto, 1880.

12 SABINE, Lorenzo. *Biographical Sketches of Loyalists of the American Revolution: With an Historical Essay.* 2 vols. Rev ed. Boston, 1864.

13 [SCHAW, Janet.] *Journal of a Lady of Quality: Being the Narrative of a Journey from Scotland to the West Indies, North Carolina, and Portugal, in the Years 1774 to 1776.* Eds. Evangeline W. and Charles M. Andrews. New Haven, 1921.

14 SCOTT, Kenneth. "Tory Associators of Portsmouth [N.H.]." *Wm Mar Q*, 3d ser., XVII (1960), 507-515.

15 SIEBERT, Wilbur H. "The Dispersion of the American Tories." *Miss Val Hist Rev*, I (1914), 185-197.

16 SIEBERT, Wilbur H. "East Florida as a Refuge of Southern Loyalists, 1774-1785." *Proc Am Ant Soc*, n.s., XXXVII (1928), 226-246.

17 SIEBERT, Wilbur H. "George Washington and the Loyalists." *Proc Am Ant Soc*, n.s., XLII (1933), 49-115.

18 SIEBERT, Wilbur H. "Kentucky's Struggle with Its Loyalist Proprietors." *Miss Val Hist Rev*, VII (1920), 113-126.

19 SIEBERT, Wilbur H. "The Loyalists and the Six Nation Indians in the Niagara Peninsula." *Trans Roy Soc Canad*, 3d ser., IX (1915), 79-128.

20 SIEBERT, Wilbur H. "The Loyalists in West Florida and the Natchez District." *Miss Val Hist Rev*, II (1916), 465-483.

1 SIEBERT, Wilbur H. *The Loyalists of Pennsylvania.* Columbus, Ohio, 1920.

2 SMITH, Jonathan. "Toryism in Worcester County During the War for Independence." *Proc Mass Hist Soc*, XLVIII (1915), 15-25.

3 SMITH, Paul H. "The American Loyalists: Notes on Their Organization and Numerical Strength." *Wm Mar Q*, 3d ser., XXV (1968), 259-277.

4 SPIRO, Robert H., Jr. "John Loudon McAdam in Revolutionary New York." *N-Y Hist Soc Q*, XL (1956), 28-54.

5 STANLEY, George F. S. "The Six Nations and the American Revolution." *Ontario Hist*, LVI (1964), 217-232.

6 STARK, James H. *The Loyalists of Massachusetts and the Other Side of the American Revolution.* Boston, 1910.

7 STOUDT, John J. "The German Press in Pennsylvania and the American Revolution." *Pa Mag Hist*, LIX (1935), 74-90.

8 THOMPSON, James W. "Anti-Loyalist Legislation During the American Revolution." *Ill Law Rev*, III (1908), 81-90, 147-171.

9 THORNE, Dorothy Gilbert. "North Carolina Friends and the Revolution." *N C Hist Rev*, XXXVIII (1961), 323-340.

10 TRYON, Winthrop P. "Whig Strategy on the Dutchess County Border; The Work of the Fredericksburg Precinct Committee and the New York Provincial Committee in Checking Tory Activities (1776-1777)." *Bull N-Y Hist Soc*, VI (1923), 111-127.

11 TYLER, Moses C. "The Party of the Loyalists in the American Revolution." *Am Hist Rev*, I (1895), 24-45.

12 VAN TYNE, Claude H. *The Loyalists in the American Revolution.* New York, 1902.

13 VERMEULE, Cornelius C. "The Active Loyalists of New Jersey." *Proc N H Hist Soc*, LII (1934), 87-95.

14 WALLACE, William S. *The United Empire Loyalists; A Chronicle of the Great Migration.* Toronto, 1914.

15 WARD, A Gertrude. "John Ettwein and the Moravians in the Revolution." *Pa Hist*, I (1934), 191-201.

16 ZEICHNER, Oscar. "The Rehabilitation of Loyalists in Connecticut." *N Eng Q*, XI (1938), 308-330.

C. WARTIME DISRUPTION

17 BARCK, Oscar T. *New York City During the War for Independence.* New York, 1931.

18 BLUMENTHAL, Walter H. *Women Camp Followers of the American Revolution.* Philadelphia, 1952.

19 CAMPBELL, William W. *Annals of Tryon County; or, the Border Warfare of New York.* New York, 1831.

1 COMETTI, Elizabeth. "Inflation in Revolutionary Maryland." *Wm Mar Q*, 3d ser., VIII (1951), 228-234.

2 COMETTI, Elizabeth. "Women in the Revolution." *N Eng Q*, XX (1947), 329-346.

3 FITHIAN, Philip Vickers. *Journal, 1775-1776, Written on the Virginia-Pennsylvania Frontier and in the Army Around New York.* Eds. R. G. Albion and L. Dodson. Princeton, 1934.

4 GRAY, Robert. "Colonel Robert Gray's Observations on the War in Carolina." *S C Hist Mag*, XI (1910), 139-159.

5 HAMILTON, Mary S. "Elmsford and the Neutral Ground." *Bull Westchester County Hist Soc*, X (1934), 51-56, 83-90.

6 HARLOW, Ralph V. "Economic Conditionns in Massachusetts During the American Revolution." With remarks by Samuel E. Morison. *Pub Col Soc Mass*, XX (1920), 163-192.

7 HART, Freeman H. *The Valley of Virginia in the American Revolution, 1763-1789.* Chapel Hill, 1942.

8 HILDRUP, R. L. "The Salt Supply of North Carolina During the American Revolution." *N C Hist Rev*, XXII (1945), 393-417.

9 HUFELAND, Otto. *Westchester County During the American Revolution, 1775-1783.* New York, 1926.

10 JENSEN, Merrill. "The American Revolution and American Agriculture." With comment by Wayne D. Rasmussen. *Ag Hist*, LXIII (1969), 107-127.

11 KENNEY, Alice P. "The Albany Dutch: Loyalists and Patriots." *N Y Hist*, XLII (1961), 331-350.

12 LEFLER, Hugh T., and Paul WAGER, eds. *Orange County, 1752-1952.* Chapel Hill, 1953.

13 LEIBY, Adrian C. *The Revolutionary War in the Hackensack Valley: The Jersey Dutch and the Neutral Ground, 1775-1783.* New Brunswick, 1962.

14 LEWIS, Anthony M. "Jefferson and Virginia's Frontiers, 1774-1781." *Miss Val Hist Rev*, XXXIV (1948), 551-588.

15 LITTLE, Mrs. William S. "The Massacre of Cherry Valley." *Pub Roch Hist Soc*, VI (1927), 99-128.

16 MC GOWEN, George S., Jr. "The Charles Town Board of Police, 1780-1782: A Study in Civil Administration Under Military Occupation." *Proc S C Hist Assn* (1964), 25-42.

17 MASON, Bernard. "Entrepreneurial Activity in New York During the American Revolution." *Bus Hist Rev*, XL (1966), 190-212. See 109.16.

18 MATHER, Frederic G. *The Refugees of 1776 from Long Island to Connecticut.* Albany, 1913.

19 MISHOFF, Willard O. "Business in Philadelphia During the British Occupation, 1777-1778." *Pa Mag Hist*, LXI (1937), 165-181.

1 MORRIS, Francis G. and Phyllis M. "Economic Conditions in North Carolina About 1780." *N C Hist Rev*, XVI (1939), 107-133, 296-327.

2 NASH, Willis G. "The Burning of Kingston." *Proc Ulster County Hist Soc for 1933-1934*, 51-60.

3 RILEY, Edward M. "Yorktown During the Revolution." *Va Mag Hist*, LVII (1949), 22-43, 176-188, 274,285.

4 STOESEN, Alexander R. "The British Occupation of Charleston, 1780-1782." *S C Hist Mag*, LXII (1962), 71-82.

5 THURSFIELD, Hugh. "Smallpox in the American War of Independence." *Ann Med Hist*, 3d ser., II (1940), 312-318.

6 WIENER, Frederick B. *Civilians Under Military Justice: The British Practice Since 1689, Especially in North America.* Chicago, 1967.

D. THE EXTENT OF REVOLUTIONARY CHANGE

7 BROWN, Richard D. "The Confiscation and Disposition of Loyalists' Estates in Suffolk County, Massachusetts. *Wm Mar Q*, 3d ser., XXI (1964), 534-550.

8 BROWN, Robert E. "Economic Democracy Before the Constitution." *Am Q*, VII (1955), 257-276.

9 CHYET, Stanley F. "The Political Rights of the Jews in the United States, 1776-1840." *Am Jew Arch*, IX (1958), 14-75.

10 COLEMAN, John M. "The Impact of the American Revolution on the Governor's Councillors [of Pennsylvania]." *Pa Hist*, XXXIV (1967), 131-146.

11 CRARY, Catherine S. "Forfeited Loyalist Lands in the Western District of New York—Albany and Tryon Counties." *N Y Hist*, XXXV (1954), 239-258.

12 CREVECOEUR, Hector St. John de. *Letters from an American Farmer . . . Conveying Some Idea of the Late and Present Interior Circumstances of the British Colonies in North America.* London, 1782.†

13 CUSHING, John D. "The Cushing Court and the Abolition of Slavery in Massachusetts: More Notes on the 'Quock Walker Case.'" *Am J Leg Hist*, V (1961), 118-144.

14 DAVIS, Andrew M. "The Confiscation Laws of Massachusetts." *Pub Col Soc Mass*, VIII (1906), 50-72.

15 DOUGLASS, Elisha P. *Rebels and Democrats: The Struggle for Equal Political Rights and Majority Rule During the American Revolution.* Chapel Hill, 1955.†

16 EAST, Robert A. "The Business Entrepreneur in a Changing Colonial Economy, 1763-1795." *J Econ Hist*, VI Supp. (1946), 16-27.

17 FEER, Robert A. "Imprisonment for Debt in Massachusetts Before 1800." *Miss Val Hist Rev*, XLVIII (1961), 252-269.

1 FOX, Dixon R. "Culture in Knapsacks." *N-Y St Hist Assn J*, XI (1930), 31-52.

2 GREENE, John C. "The American Debate on the Negro's Place in Nature, 1780-1815." *J Hist Ideas*, XV (1954), 384-396.

3 HEALE, M. J. "Humanitarianism in the Early Republic: The Moral Reformers of New York, 1776-1825." *J Am Stud*, II (1968), 161-175.

4 JAMES, Sydney V. "The Impact of the American Revolution on Quakers' Ideas About Their Sect." *Wm Mar Q*, 3d ser., XIX (1962), 360-382.

5 JAMESON, J. Franklin. *The American Revolution Considered as a Social Movement*. Princeton, 1926.†

6 TOLLES, Frederick B. "The American Revolution Considered as a Social Movement: A Re-evaluation." *Am Hist Rev*, LX (1954-1955), 1-12.

7 KATES, Don B., Jr. "Abolition, Deportation, Integration: Attitudes Toward Slavery in the Early Republic." *J Neg Hist*, LIII (1968), 33-47.

8 LAMBERT, Robert S. "The Confiscation of Loyalist Property in Georgia, 1782-1786." *Wm Mar Q*, 3d ser., XX (1963), 80-94.

9 LEWIS, Orlando F. *The Development of American Prisons and Prison Customs, 1776-1845*. Albany, 1922.

10 LOFTON, John M., Jr. "Enslavement of the Southern Mind: 1775-1825." *J Neg Hist*, XLIII (1958), 132-139.

11 LUTZ, Paul V. "Land Grants for Service in the Revolution." *N-Y Hist Soc Q*, XLVIII (1964), 221-235.

12 MC COLLEY, Robert. *Slavery and Jeffersonian Virginia*. Urbana, Ill., 1964.

13 MAIER, Pauline. "The Charleston Mob and the Evolution of Popular Politics in Revolutionary South Carolina, 1765-1784." *Prospectives in American History*, IV (1970), 173-196.

14 MAIN, Jackson T. "The Distribution of Property in Post-Revolutionary Virginia." *Miss Val Hist Rev*, XLI (1954), 241-258.

15 MAIN, Jackson T. "Government by the People: The American Revolution and the Democratization of the Legislatures." *Wm Mar Q*, 3d ser., XXIII (1966), 391-407.

16 MAIN, Jackson T. "The Results of the American Revolution Reconsidered." *Historian*, XXXI (1969), 539-554.

17 MILLER, William. "The Effects of the American Revolution on Indentured Servitude." *Pa Hist*, VII (1940), 131-141.

18 MOSS, Simeon F. "The Persistence of Slavery and Involuntary Servitude in a Free State (1685-1866)." *J Neg Hist*, XXXV (1950' 289-314.

19 O'BRIEN, William. "Did the Jennison Case Outlaw Slavery in Massachusetts?" *Wm Mar Q*, 3d ser., XVII (1960), 219-241.

1 REUBENS, Beatrice G. "Pre-Emptive Rights in the Disposition of a Confiscated Estate: Philipsburgh Manor, New York." *Wm Mar Q*, 3d ser., XXII (1965), 435-456.

2 RICCARDS, Michael P. "Patriots and Plunderers: Confiscation of Loyalists' Lands in New Jersey, 1776-1786." *N J Hist*, LXXVI (1968), 14-28.

3 SINGLETON, Marvin K. "New Light on the Chancery Side of Virginia's Evolution to Statehood." *J Am Stud*, II (1968), 149-160.

4 SPECTOR, Robert M. "The Quock Walker Cases (1781-83)—Slavery, Its Abolition, and Negro Citizenship in Early Massachusetts." *J Neg Hist*, LIII (1968), 12-32.

5 VER STEEG, Clarence. "The American Revolution Considered as an Economic Movement." *Hunt Lib Q*, XX (1957), 361-372.

6 VIVIAN, Jean H. "Military Land Bounties During the Revolutionary and Confederation Periods." *Md Hist Mag*, LXI (1966), 231-256.

7 WRIGHT, Benjamin F. *Consensus and Continuity, 1776-1787.* Boston, 1958. See 108.5.

8 YOSHPE, Harry B. *The Disposition of Loyalist Estates in the Southern District of the State of New York.* New York, 1939.

9 ZILVERSMIT, Arthur. *The First Emancipation: The Abolition of Slavery in the North.* Chicago, 1967.

10 ZILVERSMIT, Arthur. "Quok Walker, Mumbet, and the Abolition of Slavery in Massachusetts." *Wm Mar Q*, 3d ser., XXV (1968), 614-624.

IX. Revolutionary Equilibrium in the Postwar Era

1. The Aftermath of War

11 BOYD, Julian P. "Attempts to Form New States in New York and Pennsylvania, 1786-1796." *N Y St Hist Assn Q J*, XII (1931), 257-270.

12 BURNETT, Edmund C. "The Committee of the States, 1784." *Ann Rep Am Hist Assn*, I (1913), 141-158.

13 CABELL, N. F. "Some Fragments of an Intended Report on the Post-Revolutionary History of Agriculture in Virginia." *Wm Mar Q*, XXVI (1918), 145-168.

14 COLEMAN, Kenneth. "Federal Indian Relations in the South, 1781-1789." *Chron Okla*, XXXV (1958), 435-458.

15 DAVIES, Wallace E. "The Society of the Cincinnati in New England 1783-1800." *Wm Mar Q*, 3d ser., V (1948), 3-25. See 111.9.

16 DAVIS, Andrew M. "The Shays Rebellion, a Political Aftermath." *Proc Am Ant Soc*, XXI (1911), 57-79.

1 DECONDE, Alexander. "William Vans Murray's *Political Sketches*: A Defense of the American Experiment." *Miss Val Hist Rev*, XLI (1955), 623-640.

2 DYER, Walter A. "Embattled Farmers." *N Eng Q*, IV (1931), 460-481.

3 ELLSWORTH, Lucius F. "The Philadelphia Society for the Promotion of Agriculture and Agricultural Reform, 1785-1793." *Ag Hist*, XLII (1968), 189-199.

4 FEER, Robert A. "Shays's Rebellion and the Constitution: A Study in Causation." *N Eng Q*, XLII (1969), 388-410.

5 FISKE, John. *The Critical Period of American History, 1783-89*. Boston, 1888.

6 GODECHOT, Jacques L. "Les Relations Economiques entre la France et les Etats-Unis de 1778 à 1789." *French Hist Stud*, I (1958), 26-39.

7 HOUTTE, Hubert van, ed. "American Commercial Conditions, and Negotiations with Austria, 1783-1786." *Am Hist Rev*, XVI (1911), 567-587.

8 HUME, Edgar E. "Early Opposition to the Cincinnati." *Am*, XXX (1936), 597-638.

9 JENSEN, Merrill. "The Creation of the National Domain, 1781-1784." *Miss Val Hist Rev*, XXVI (1939), 323-342.

10 JENSEN, Merrill. *The New Nation: A History of the United States During the Confederation, 1781-1789*. New York, 1950.†

11 JOHNSON, Herbert A. "Toward a Reappraisal of the 'Federal' Government: 1783-1789." *Am J Leg Hist*, VIII (1964), 314-325.

12 KAPLAN, Sidney. "Pay, Pension, and Power: Economic Grievances of the Massachusetts Officers of the Revolution." *Bos Pub Lib Q*, III (1951), 15-34, 127-142.

13 KAPLAN, Sidney. "Veteran Officers and Politics in Massachusetts, 1783-1787." *Wm Mar Q*, 3d ser., IX (1952), 29-57.

14 KOHN, Richard H. *The Federalists and the Army: Politics and the Birth of the Military Establishment, 1783-1795*. Ph.D. thesis, U of Wisconsin, 1968.

15 KOHN, Richard H. "The Inside History of the Newburgh Conspiracy: America and the Coup d'Etat." *Wm Mar Q*, 3d ser., XXVII (1970), 187-220.

16 LAMBERT, Robert S. "The Repossession of Georgia, 1782-1784." *Proc S C Hist Assn 1957*, 14-25.

17 MC LAUGHLIN, Andrew C. *The Confederation and the Constitution, 1783-1789*. New York, 1905.†

18 MAIN, Jackson T. "Political Parties in Revolutionary Maryland, 1780-1787." *Md Hist Mag*, LXII (1967), 1-27.

1 MAIN, Jackson T. "Sections and Politics in Virginia, 1781-1787." *Wm Mar Q*, 3d ser., XII (1955), 96-112.

2 MINOT, George R. *History of the Insurrection in Massachusetts in 1786*. 2d ed. Boston, 1810.

3 FEER, Robert A. "George Richard Minot's *History of the Insurrection*: History, Propaganda, and Autobiography." *N Eng Q*, XXXV (1962), 203-228.

4 MOODY, R. E. "Samuel Ely: Forerunner of Shays." *N Eng Q*, V (1932), 105-134.

5 MORGAN, Edmund S., ed. "The Political Establishments of the United States, 1784." *Wm Mar Q*, 3d ser., XXIII (1966), 286-308.

6 MORRIS, Richard B. "The Confederation Period and the American Historian." *Wm Mar Q*, 3d ser., XIII (1956), 139-156.

7 MORRIS, Richard B. "Insurrection in Massachusetts." In *America in Crisis*, ed. Daniel Aaron. New York, 1952.

8 NUSSBAUM, Frederick L. "American Tobacco and French Politics, 1783-1789." *Pol Sci Q*, XL (1925), 497-516.

9 RICH, Myra L. "Speculations on the Significance of Debt: Virginia, 1781-1789." *Va Mag Hist*, LXXVI (1968).

10 SCHAFFER, Alan. "Virginia's 'Critical Period.'" In *The Old Dominion*, ed. D. B. Rutman. Charlottesville, Va., 1964.

11 SMITH, Jonathan. "The Depression 1785 and Daniel Shays's Rebellion." *Wm Mar Q*, 3d ser., V (1948), 77-94.

12 STOVER, John F. "French-American Trade During the Confederation." *N C Hist Rev*, XXXV (1958), 399-414.

13 TATTER, Henry. "State and Federal Land Policy During the Confederation Period." *Ag Hist*, IX (1935), 176-186.

14 TAYLOR, Robert J. "Trial at Trenton." *Wm Mar Q*, 3d ser., XXVI (1969), 521-547.

15 WARREN, Joseph P. "The Confederation and the Shays Rebellion." *Am Hist Rev*, XI (1905), 42-67.

16 WILSON, Janet. "The Bank of North America and Pennsylvania Politics: 1781-1787." *Pa Mag Hist*, LXVI (1942), 3-28.

17 ZEICHNER, Oscar. "The Loyalist Problem in New York After the Revolution." *N Y Hist*, XXI (1940), 284-302.

18 ZORNOW, William F. "Massachusetts Tariff Policies, 1775-1789." *Essex Inst Hist Coll*, XC (1954), 194-215.

19 ZORNOW, William F. "New York Tariff Policies, 1775-1789." *N Y Hist*, XXXVII (1956), 40-63.

20 ZORNOW, William F. "Tariff Policies in South Carolina, 1775-1789." *S C Hist Mag*, LVI (1955), 31-44.

21 ZORNOW, William F. "The Tariff Policies of Virginia, 1775-1789." *Va Mag Hist*, LXXII (1954), 306-319.

2. The Achievement of Stability

A. THE REORGANIZATION OF GOVERNMENT

1 ADAIR, Douglass. "The Tenth Federalist Revisited." *Wm Mar Q*, 3d ser., VIII (1951), 48-67.

2 ADAMS, Willi Paul. *Republikanismus and die ersten Einzelstaatsverfassungen; Zur ideengeschichtlichen and verfassungsgeschichtlichen Komponente der amerikanischen Revolution, 1775-1780.* Berlin, 1968.

3 BEARD, Charles A. *An Economic Interpretation of the Constitution of the United States.* New York, 1913.†

4 BROGAN, Denis W. "The Quarrel over Charles Austin Beard and the American Constitution." *Econ Hist Rev*, 2d ser., XVIII (1965), 199-223.

5 CORWIN, Edward S. "The Progress of Constitutional Theory Between the Declaration of Independence and the Meeting of the Philadelphia Convention." *Am Hist Rev*, XXX (1925), 511-536.

6 EIDELBERG, Paul. *The Philosophy of the Constitution: A Reinterpretation of the Founding Fathers.* New York, 1968.†

7 ELKINS, Stanley, and Eric MC KITRICK. "The Founding Fathers: Young Men of the Revolution." *Pol Sci Q*, LXXVI (1961), 181-216.

8 FARRAND, Max. *The Framing of the Constitution of the United States.* New Haven, 1913.†

9 FERGUSON, E. James. "The Nationalists of 1781-1783 and the Economic Interpretation of the Constitution." *J Am Hist*, LVI (1969), 241-261. See 81.5.

10 KENYON, Cecelia M. "Men of Little Faith: The Anti-Federalists on the Nature of Representative Government." *Wm Mar Q*, 3d ser., XII (1955), 3-43.

11 KENYON, Cecelia M., ed. *The Antifederalists.* Indianapolis, 1966.†

12 LIBBY, Orin G. *Georgraphical Distribution of the Vote . . . on the . . . Constitution.* Madison, 1894.

13 LYND, Staughton. "The Compromise of 1787." *Pol Sci Q*, LXXI (1966), 225-250.

14 MC DONALD, Forrest. *E Pluribus Unum: The Formation of the American Republic. 1776-1790.* Boston, 1965.†

15 MC DONALD, Forrest. *We the People: The Economic Origins of the Constitution.* Chicago, 1958.†

16 MAIN, Jackson T. *The Antifederalists: Critics of the Constitution, 1781-1788.* Chapel Hill, 1961.†

17 MAIN, Jackson T. "Chalres A. Beard and the Constitution: A Critical Review of Forrest McDonald's *We the People.*" With a rebuttal by Forrest McDonald. *Wm Mar Q*, 3d ser., XVII (1960), 86-110.

1 MASON, Alpheus T. "The Federalist—A Split Personality." *Am Hist Rev*, LVII (1952), 625-643.

2 RUTLAND, Robert A. *The Birth of the Bill of Rights, 1776-1791.* Chapel Hill, 1955.

3 RUTLAND, Robert A. *The Ordeal of the Constitution: The Anti-Federalists and the Ratification Struggle of 1787-1788.* Norman, Okla., 1966.

4 SCHUYLER, Robert L. "Agreement in the Federal Convention." *Pol Sci Q*, XXI (1916), 289-299.

5 THOMAS, Robert E. "A Reappraisal of Charles A. Beard's *An Economic Interpretation of the Constitution of the United States*." *Am Hist Rev*, LVII (1952), 370-375.

6 THOMAS, Robert E. "The Virginia Convention of 1788: A Criticism of Beard's *An Economic Interpretation of the Constitution*." *J S Hist*, XIX (1953), 63-72.

7 WEBSTER, William C. "Comparative Study of the State Constitution of the American Revolution." American Academy of Political and Social Science *Annals*, IX (1897), 380-420.

8 WHITE, Leonard D. *The Federalists; A Study in Administrative History.* New York, 1948.†

9 WOOD, Gordon S. *The Creation of the American Republic, 1776-1787.* Chapel Hill, 1969.†

B. THE ECONOMIC BASIS OF STABILITY

10 BATES, Whitney K. "Northern Speculators and Southern State Debts: 1790." *Wm Mar Q*, 3d ser., XIX (1962), 30-48.

11 BJORK, Gordon C. "The Weaning of the American Economy: Independence, Market Changes, and Economic Development." *J Econ Hist*, XXIV (1964), 541-560.

12 BRUCHEY, Stuart W. *Robert Oliver, Merchant of Baltimore, 1783-1819.* Baltimore, 1956.

13 BRUCHEY, Stuart W. "Success and Failure Factors: American Merchants in Foreign Trade in the Eighteenth and Early Nineteenth Centuries. *Bus Hist Rev*, XXXII (1958), 272-292.

14 COATSWORTH, John H. "American Trade with European Colonies in the Caribbean and South America, 1790-1812." *Wm Mar Q*, 3d ser., XXIV (1967), 243-266.

15 COLLES, Christopher, *A Study of the Roads of the United States of America, 1789.* Ed. W. W. Ristow. Cambridge, Mass., 1961.

16 EAST, Robert A. *Business Enterprise in the American Revolutionary Era.* London and New York, 1938. See 102.17.

17 ELAZER, Daniel J. "Banking and Federalism in the Early American Republic." si,Hunt Lib Q, *XXVIII (1965), 301-320.*

1 HAMMOND, Bray. *Banks and Politics in America from the Revolution to the Civil War*. Princeton, 1957.†

2 NETTELS, Curtis P. *The Emergence of a National Economy, 1775, 1815.* New York, 1962.†

3 RASCH, Aa. "American Trade in the Baltic, 1783-1807." *Scandinavian Economic History Review*, XIII (1965), 31-64.

4 VAN FENSTERMAKER, J. "The Statistics of American Commercial Banking, 1782-1818." *J Econ Hist*, XXV (1965), 400-413.

5 BARNBY, H. G. *The Prisoners of Algiers: An Account of the Forgotten American-Algerian War, 1785-1797*. London, 1966.

C. THE INTERNATIONAL BASIS OF STABILITY

American-Algerian War, 1785-1797. London, 1966.

6 BEMIS, Samuel F. *Jay's Treaty: A Study in Commerce and Diplomacy*. New York, 1923.†

7 BEMIS, Samuel F. *Pinckney's Treaty: America's Advantage from Europe's Distress, 1783-1800*. Baltimore, 1926; new ed. New Haven, 1960.

8 BOWMAN, Albert H. "Jefferson, Hamilton, and American Foreign Policy." *Pol Sci Q*, LXXI (1956), 18-41.

9 BOYD, Julian P. *Number 7: Alexander Hamilton's Secret Attempt to Control American Foreign Policy, with Supporting Documents*. Princeton, 1964.

10 BREBNER, John B. *The North Atlantic Triangle: The Interplay of Canada, the United States, and Great Britain*. New Haven, 1945.

11 DECONDE, Alexander. *Entangling Alliance: Politics and Diplomacy Under George Washington*. Durham, N.C., 1958.

12 DORSEY, Rhoda M. "The Pattern of Baltimore Commerce During the Confederation Period." *Md Hist Mag*, LXII (1967). 119-134.

13 FIELD, James A., Jr. *America and the Mediterranean World, 1776-1882.* Princeton, 1969.

14 FRASER, Leon. *English Opinion of the American Constitution and Government (1783-1798)*. New York, 1915.

15 GILBERT, Felix. *To the Farewell Address: Ideas of Early American Foreign Policy. sm,Princeton, 1961.†*

16 PERKINS, Bradford. *The First Rapprochement: England and the United States, 1795-1805*. Philadelphia, 1955.

17 PETERSON, Merrill D. "Thomas Jefferson and Commercial Policy, 1783-1793." *Wm Mar Q*, 3d ser., XXII (1965), 584-610.

18 RITCHESON, Charles R. "Anglo-American Relations, 1783-1794." *S Atl Q*, LVIII (1959), 364-380.

19 WHITAKER, Arthur P. *The Spanish-American Frontier: 1783-1795.* Boston and New York, 1927.†

D. THE POLITICAL AND CULTURAL BASES OF STABILITY

1 BALDWIN, Leland D. *Whiskey Rebels; The Story of a Frontier Uprising.* Pittsburgh, 1939.†

2 BARKER, Howard F., and M. L. HANSEN. "Report of Committee on Linguistic and National Stocks in the Population of the United States in 1790." *Ann Rep Am Hist Assn*, I (1931), 103-441.

3 BOORSTIN, Daniel J. *The Lost World of Thomas Jefferson.* New York, 1948.†

4 CALHOUN, Daniel H. *Professional Lives in America: Structure and Aspiration, 1750-1850.* Cambridge, Mass., 1954.

5 CHARLES, Joseph. *The Origins of the American Party System.* Williamsburg, 1956.†

6 COOKE, Jacob E. "The Whiskey Insurrection: A Re-evaluation." *Pa Hist*, XXX (1963), 316-346.

7 CUNNINGHAM, Noble E., Jr. *The Jeffersonian Republicans: The Formation of Party Organization, 1789-1801.* Chapel Hill, 1958.†

8 DAUER, Manning J. *The Adams Federalists.* Baltimore, 1953.†

9 DUNBAR, Louise B. *A Study of "Monarchical" Tendencies in the United States, from 1776 to 1801.* Urbana, Ill., 1922.

10 FISCHER, David H. *The Revolution of American Conservatism: The Federalist Party in the Era of Jeffersonian Democracy.* New York, 1965.†

11 GRISWOLD, Rufus W. *The Republican Court, or American Society in the Days of Washington.* Rev. ed. New York, 1864.

12 HOFSTADTER, Richard. *The Idea of a Party System: The Rise of Legitimate Opposition in the United States, 1780-1840.* Berkeley, 1969.†

13 HOWE, John R. "Republican Thought and the Political Violence of the 1790s." *Am Q*, XIX (1967), 147-165.

14 INGERSOLL, David E. "Machiavelli and Madison: Perspectives on Political Stability." *Pol Sci Q*, LXXXV (1970), 259-280.

15 KOCH, G. Adolph. *Republican Religion; the American Revolution and the Cult of Reason.* New York, 1933.†

16 LEVY, Leonard W. *Jefferson and Civil Liberties: The Darker Side.* Cambridge, Mass., 1963.

17 MC LOUGHLIN, William G. "The Balkcom Case (1782) and the Pietistic Theory of Separation of Church and State." *Wm Mar Q*, 3d ser., XXIV (1967), 267-283.

18 MANNING, William. *The Key of Libberty, Shewing the Causes Why a Free Government Has Always Failed, and a Remidy Against It; Written in Year 1798.* Ed. Samuel E. Morison. Billerica, Mass., 1922; repr. in *Wm Mar Q*, 3d ser., XIII (1956), 202-254.

1 MILLER, William. "The Democratic Societies and the Whiskey Insurrection." *Pa Mag Hist*, LXII (1938), 324-349.

2 NAGEL, Paul C. *One Nation Indivisible: The Union in American Thought, 1776-1861*. New York, 1964.

3 NASH, Gary B. "The American Clergy and the French Revolution." *Wm Mar Q*, 3d ser., XXII (1965), 392-412.

4 RANNEY, John C. "The Bases of American Federalism." *Wm Mar Q*, 3d ser., III (1946), 1-35.

5 SMELSER, Marshall. "The Federalist Period as an Age of Passion." *Am Q*, X (1958), 391-419.

6 SMELSER, Marshall. "The Jacobin Phrenzy: The Menace of Monarchy, Plutocracy, and Anglophilia, 1789-1798." *Rev Pol*, XXI (1959), 239-258.

7 SPILLER, Robert E. *The Americans in England During the First Half Century of Independence*. New York, 1926.

8 STAUFFER, Vernon. *New England and the Bavarian Illuminati*. New York, 1918.

9 WARREN, Charles. *Jacobin and Junto; or, Early American Politics as Viewed in the Diary of Dr. Nathaniel Ames, 1758-1822*. Cambridge, Mass., 1931.

10 WILLIAMSON, Chilton. *American Suffrage: From Property to Democracy, 1760-1860*. Princeton, 1960.

11 WILTSE, Charles M. *The Jeffersonian Tradition in American Democracy*. Chapel Hill, 1935.†

X. The Revolution in Comparative Perspective

12 AMANN, Peter. "Revolution: A Redefinition." *Pol Sci Q*, LXXVII (1962), 36-53.

13 ARENDT, Hannah. *On Revolution*. New York, 1963.†

14 BRINTON, Crane. *The Anatomy of Revolution*. New York, 1938.†

15 EISENSTADT, S. N. *The Political Systems of Empires*. London, 1963.

16 KIRCHEIMER, Otto. "Confirming Conditions and Revolutionary Breakthroughs." *Am Pol Sci Rev*, LIX (1965), 964-974.

17 KOHT, Halvdan. "The American Revolution as a European Revolution." In *The American Spirit in Europe*. Philadelphia, 1949.

18 LIPSET, Seymour M. *The First New Nation: The United States in Historical and Comparative Perspective*. New York, 1963.†

1 LIPSET, Seymour M. "The 'Newness' of the New Nation." In *The Comparative Approach to American History*, ed. C. Vann Woodward. New York, 1968.

2 MORRIS, Richard B. *The Emerging Nations and the American Revolution.* New York, 1970.

3 NELSON, William H. "The Revolutionary Character of the American Revolution." *Am Hist Rev*, LXX (1965), 998-1014.

4 PALMER, Robert R. *The Age of the Democratic Revolution: A Political History of Europe and America, 1760-1800.* 2 vols. Princeton, 1959-1965.†

5 PALMER, Robert R. "The Revolution." In *The Comparative Approach to American History*, ed. C. Vann Woodward. New York, 1968.†

6 POLE, J. R. *Political Representation in England and the Origins of the American Republic.* New York, 1966.

7 RUDOLPH, Lloyd L. "The Eighteenth Century Mob in Europe and America." *Am Q*, XI (1959), 447-469.

8 SEE, Henri. *Evolution et Révolution.* Paris, 1929, pp. 71-114.

9 STONE, Lawrence. "Theories of Revolution." *W Pol*, XVIII (1966), 159-176.

NOTES

INDEX

B

122

INDEX

INDEX

INDEX

INDEX

INDEX

INDEX

INDEX

133

INDEX